Whitetail Success By Design
Designing your next hunt of a lifetime

by

Jeff Sturgis

Edited by
Mavis Sturgis and Michael Bey

Copyright © 2012 by
Jeffrey R. Sturgis

All rights reserved. No part of this publication may be reproduced, distributed, or transmitted in any form or by any means, including photocopying, recording, or other electronic or mechanical methods, without the prior written permission of the publisher, except in the case of brief quotations embodied in critical reviews and certain other noncommercial uses permitted by copyright law. For permission requests, write to the publisher, addressed "Attention: Permissions Coordinator," at the address below.

Whitetail Habitat Solutions, LLC
PO Box 536
Munising, MI 49862
www.whitetailhabitatsolutions.com

Ordering Information:
Quantity sales. Special discounts are available on quantity purchases by corporations, associations, and others. For details, contact the publisher at the address above.

Orders by U.S. trade bookstores and wholesalers. Whitetail Habitat Solutions, LLC: Tel: (906) 630-3105; or visit: www.whitetailhabitatsolutions.com

All photos used in this publication were provided by the author, or used by permission from the following individuals, including: Doug Ward, John Komp, Ross Fernandez, and Matt Grucz.

Printed in the United States of America
ISBN 978-0-9882900-0-6

Dedication

During nearly three decades of hunting whitetails, I have accumulated some incredible memories while hunting with both family and friends. Making memories to last a lifetime is a huge part of what I feel the tradition of hunting is about. Although my children are still young, the memories I have while hunting with them will truly be with me for the rest of my life.

To Sammy: Lying on the floor of Grandpa's blind with your brother, or cuddled into my arms as the snow fell around us and your little face looked up at me through 2 facemasks and a knit hat...while you slept! Have you ever stayed awake in the blind? Your patience and peace while spending time with me was precious and sweet.

To Autumn: It was the last minute of shooting light, the last day of MI's firearm season. You were an adventurous 5 years old, but probably a little nervous and scared in the fading light. The sudden "BOOM" of the rifle didn't help to calm your spirit! But the hours following were filled with the excitement we both shared, realizing that we were in the blind together, as I shot the largest buck I had ever taken in MI.

To Jake: Hunts in MI, PA, WI...and more yet to come. It was in PA after an hour walk to the home-made blind in the dark, and after several hours of sitting in both rain and snow. It was calm, cold, quiet and you never complained, but instead, only looked up at me and said, "Daddy I love you".

You guys are always in my many thoughts and prayers while sitting alone in a tree stand, in some woodlot, in some state. You are in my thoughts, passion and smiles while writing late at night or driving to my next hunt or client. Each one of you offers a special personality of happiness, love and drive that fuels all I do, and the many hunting memories that are being built along the way are better whether you are in the blind with me, or not. Sammy, Autumn and Jake I love you!

10/07/10 07:01PM

Table of Contents

Dedication II
Acknowledgement..V
Foreword by Tony Smith..VII

Chapter 1	Introduction 11

Goals
Chapter 2	Design Goals 15

Structure
Chapter 3	Analyzing the Framework of the Land You Hunt 21
Chapter 4	Road Kill Map to Habitat Success............................ 33
Chapter 5	Hide and Seek Habitat Changes 39
Chapter 6	Define and Conquer 45
Chapter 7	Depth of Cover 51
Chapter 8	Low Stress Deer Parcels = Low Stress Deer Herds 59

Critical Concepts of High Quality Habitat and Hunting Designs
Chapter 9	Paralleling Habitat Features 69
Chapter 10	Lines of Deer Movement 75
Chapter 11	High Powered Buck Travel Corridors 83
Chapter 12	Habitat Stem Per Acre... 89

Pictorial Tips and Tactics.. 95

Chapter 13	Screening Cover 111
Chapter 14	Bedding Layers for Mature Bucks and Does.......... 117
Chapter 15	High Powered Cool Season Bedding Areas 123
Chapter 16	Balance Diagnosis of Food and Cover 135
Chapter 17	Building Part Time Deer Herds.............................. 145
Chapter 18	Establishing Patterns of Food Plot Use................. 151

The Next Step: Hunting and Harvesting Mature Bucks
Chapter 19	Predatory Access... 155
Chapter 20	Stand Stories 161
Chapter 21	The Morning Sneak 167
Chapter 22	Conclusion... 173

Acknowledgement

This book is a culmination of a lifetime of personal whitetail experiences. The past 27 seasons of hunting whitetails has provided me with some of the most magically beautiful memories that nature could provide. There is a God, and He has blessed me not only with enough opportunities, adventures and memories to last a lifetime, but with an ever-expanding network of individuals to share in those memories.

John Ozoga, Mark Thomas, Ed Spinazzola, and Charles Alsheimer; thank you for being the consummate whitetail professionals whom I have both looked up to and been inspired by. Brian Murphy and Lindsay Thomas of the Quality Deer Management Association; I have appreciated your continued support throughout the years by allowing me to contribute to the publication of Quality Whitetails, as well as by offering such an admirable voice of leadership and trust within the whitetail community. Jim Isleib, Alger County Extension Director; your advice and consultation in assisting me while planting food plots in completely infertile soils was a critical component of great success.

Mom and Dad, thank you for your unwavering support, love, and encouragement. For the past 42 years no matter how my life has changed, for the better or worse, you have never failed to be the exceptional team of parents and role models, teaching by example the highest degree of integrity and Christian values. Dad, I will never forget standing with Mike Pratt ¼ mile across the field from you, and watching as you sat in a tangle of fencerow grape vines and shot your first buck. And Mom, I can't thank you enough for the many hours of listening to my thoughts, encouraging me to fulfill my dreams, and praying for me.

Diane, thank you so much for not only always believing in me and being my best friend, but by also being my constant sounding board for brainstorming new ideas, book titles, pictorial sections and cover designs.

What an incredible, growing circle of hunting buddies, including: John and Mike, Dave, Robb and the late Bob P., Joe and the late Jerry L, Tim, Max, Karl and Paul, Tony AKA Big T, Ross, Tex, John L, Colin, Dave, Ben, my brother Kevin and my Dad, my cousin Brent, Skip, Jerry, Bill, and Perry. Tim, thank you for teaching me that hunting with friends is better than hunting alone. Mike, my longest hunting buddy, thank you for sharing in all of the hunting and fishing memories for the past 30 years. To Mike and Guy P, I am forever grateful for getting me into the woods when no one in my family hunted. And to Karl, a true brother in hunting with the quality of caring more about the pursuit of the deer...than who actually killed that deer.

Tony Smith - thank you for the incredible Forward, your contributions to this book, and kind words! While our hunts and times together have been limited, I can't wait for our next time in the woods together.

Michael Bey and Mom; what a great team to assist me throughout the editing process of this book. I feel extremely lucky to have had both of you helping to make my book look presentable. I have appreciated your critique as much as the many skills you both so generously brought to the table!

Leon Hank, thank you for your initial direction and consult, including the advice to seek a local printer to assist with this endeavor. Jackie and Greg from Evans Printing, you both have exceeded my expectations and are a large part of why the finished product of this book looks better than I could have imagined.

Lord willing, I will enthusiastically travel throughout the remaining years of my life while experiencing the fabric of the Whitetail Deer, which has been woven into the many cherished memories of my past. To say I have been "blessed," seems almost an understatement. So many experiences, forms of advice, family, friends and professional resources have contributed to the past 27 wonderful seasons of my personal whitetail experiences. Thank You!

Foreword

"When the student is ready the teacher will appear"
– Buddhist proverb

    If you are reading this book , you're probably either a novice deer hunter or one of us "nuts" that eats, sleeps, and breaths all things whitetail. I congratulate you on continuing your quest to learn all there is to know about the most sought after game species on the planet. The pursuit of whitetails, and the desire to know all there is to know about them, is an endless love affair, and if you believe that this book will be the end all, think again. It likely will lead to even more questions as well as a greater desire to learn. Jeff Sturgis is the consummate teacher and through this reading, and more to come, you will never drive past a "road kill" deer again without questioning "why it attempted to cross there".

    A young boy's passion for hunting whitetails was sparked at a very young age after his parents had divorced and his mother converted the first floor of their old farm house into an apartment to help pay the mortgage. The tenant, who we'll call Tom, because that's his name, recognized the boy's insatiable appetite to tag along with him when he would run rabbits with his beagle or train his Britney spaniel on pheasants in the woods and fields behind the house. One fall morning Tom happily dragged this bright eyed lad along on an archery deer hunt. While crouching behind him on a brush choked ditch bank, the boy had his first face to face encounter with the most fascinating creature on earth. The fire was lit! And, that boy was me!

    My mother eventually remarried, and my stepfather, in an effort to build a bond with me, revisited his youth and began hunting again. I killed many rabbits and squirrels under his steady hand and watchful eye; and then, at age 18, I killed my first whitetail buck, a spike, in a swamp adjoining the AuSable River in northern Michigan! My stepfather was instrumental in fanning the flame ignited by Tom, but his and Tom's limited knowledge of whitetails was all they were capable of passing on to me; but for their effort, I will be eternally grateful.

In the years that followed, I became a man and killed many deer across Michigan while hoping for a "chance" encounter with a mature buck. I spent many seasons enjoying my time afield while experiencing limited success, but also frustrated that my goals weren't being met. It wasn't until I began to seek new information from people that had the results I was after, that I began to experience my goal of consistently encountering mature whitetail bucks.

The first time I met Jeff Sturgis was during this "seeking period" when we were introduced by our mutual friend, Perry Russo, at Perry's deer hunting property in Michigan's "thumb" region. Jeff and I were both guests of Perry and his camp during that late October weekend, and while Perry spoke highly of Jeff beforehand, he hadn't let on about Jeff's incredible ability to consistently kill exceptional whitetails. Early in the weekend I'm sure Jeff realized that Perry and I and a couple other guests had some deeply entrenched habits that weren't conducive to consistently killing mature whitetails. So, his focus that weekend shifted from an opportunity to hunt, to an opportunity to teach. Sitting around the table conversing, I had my first introduction to the kind of thinking that I had been searching for. While all of us listened to what Jeff had to say, not everyone really "heard" it. The following morning I took the same route to the same stand as I had the previous day; yet nothing I viewed from the stand that day appeared the same to me. My paradigm had shifted!

Over the years Jeff and I became better friends, and I continued to absorb his knowledge as he graciously shared on internet forums and in magazine articles about the transformation of his heavily forested U.P. deer desert. Through food plotting, creating "layers," entry and exits to stands undetected, hunting outside-in, and a host of other tactics, he would eventually put himself in a position, by design, to kill mature bucks where few, if any, existed when he arrived. When Jeff later won the prestigious Al Brothers Deer Manager of the Year award from the Quality Deer Management Association, it only confirmed what I had already come to know and what other professionals in the field came to recognize as well.

As if consistently killing bucks in Michigan's heavily pressured southern farm country and sparsely populated northern cedar swamps wasn't enough, I watched as Jeff traveled to public land in equally pressured Pennsylvania, the bluff country of western Wisconsin, and the piney forests of Alabama. Jeff would return with bucks that represented the top 10% age class from each region without the aid of outfitters or locals - an impressive feat!

I consistently hear hunters ask, "What should I be looking for when shopping for good deer hunting property?" This can be a very expensive lesson if approached unarmed. This book will provide insight into what a property may hold, as well as its potential under a well laid-out plan. I know, from personal experience, that I looked past several potential parcels at very good prices because they didn't fit the conventional description of good deer dirt. As Jeff points out in this book, often "less is more." It's the future design capabilities that will determine a property's potential to produce. Often times it's not even the property that should be considered first, but the surrounding influences like neighbors, water, or topography. Simply put, a small investment of time and money in this book can pay huge dividends, and increase success down the road.

It's often easier for some to consider consistent success - luck, but that discounts all of the hard work and preparation that goes into making luck happen. There are plenty of books out there geared toward improving your chances on mature bucks - some that are geared toward growing the ultimate food plot, and others that focus on hunting specific regions of North America, but until now, little information has been focused on putting it altogether, by design, wherever the whitetail roams. You will find that once you are armed with the basic, but essential information, your expectations of killing mature whitetail bucks should heighten, at least until he walks into range and your knees shake so badly that you nearly lose all control! It's THAT feeling that we live for and that which Jeff can help you to experience on a more consistent basis, if...the student is ready.

Jeff is now in the planning stages of a hunt in Ohio's southern "hill" region, and I feel blessed to be sharing a camp with him once again. Who knows...that now older man with the childlike curiosity will more than likely learn something.

Savor the moments!

Tony Smith - Whitetail "nut" and proud QDMA member

Chapter 1

INTRODUCTION

It was a clear, cold start to the 3rd morning of MI's 2011 Firearm Season as I crossed the marsh on my way to the line of heavy spruce trees that bordered in front of the river. As I continued to the West I was hopeful that I would get a chance at the buck responsible for the giant rubs that dotted the heavy cover on 4-8" Jack Pines connecting food to my left, and bedding cover to my right. If I entered too far into the line of heavy spruce to access a blind, I would risk getting behind deer that would no doubt get a nose full of human scent. However, if I didn't enter far enough I could possibly be out of range of any interior deer movement. The marsh served as a perfect "bumper" of deer activity, meaning there was a very low chance of spooking any deer during my approach to the blind location, or as I allowed my scent to blow back into the area during the hours of daylight. With the flashlight off, the tall white pine served as the perfect silhouette against the star-filled sky to help me get my bearings for a quick and quiet approach into the tangle of cover.

As my pace slowed while entering the wall of conifer, the sound of my breathing reminded me both of the incredible stillness in the pre-morning hours, as well as the fact I should have spent a little more time getting into hunting shape during the previous 3 months. Without the aid of a light I picked my way through the conifer with a slight open ridge offering a collection of light ahead. Only 30 yards into the cover I almost ran into the tent that had been snuggled back into a "hidey-hole" of spruce trunks and a small patch of tag alder. I doubted a mature buck would get into my downwind area from my approach, preferring instead to cross upwind of me from south to north as he approached his bedding area.

This was a textbook "Mature Buck Bedding" set-up, located away from food, and behind doe family groups who experience had taught me, could be counted on to spend their daytime hours within close proximity to their preferred food sources. As I carefully zipped into the tent, I was looking forward to a long morning hunt before heading down to WI's Rifle Season opener the next day. The approach was good, the upwind line of deer movement I was hunting was strong and well defined, and a mature buck was obviously aggressively ripping up the area!

The morning light filtered into the spruce swamp from the east. As I stared south where I expected potential deer to approach from, the shadows and shade under the canopy of conifer at legal shooting light, made it difficult to pick out any movement. 7:30 passed. 8:00. I had barely had time to start getting chilled from my walk in, when at 8:10, a stick cracking under the obvious step of a deer, invaded the morning silence. I readied my gun as the long back of a large deer emerged through the spruce almost directly at me. As he lifted his head to quarter towards me over a small hump of ancient roots in the deer trail, his large, mature right main beam protruded wide and high from his giant head. He was less than 40 yards and stopped to seemingly stare right through me...

Success by Design

At the moment that mature buck was attempting to identify something odd within his home area, success was there for the taking...Game, Set, Match! After all, the kill is the easy part, right? Well, perhaps, but I have been known to somehow mess up even some of the easiest of opportunities. However, getting to the point of consistently having the opportunity to come face to face with a giant, to many, is the pinnacle of success, especially when designing your own success. Do you wait for luck to happen? Or do you make your own luck! I have found throughout my 27 years of deer hunting that the odds tilted heavily in my favor when I learned to recognize and even create my own opportunities by following a fairly strict pattern of concepts that will work anywhere a whitetail roams.

The concept of designing your next hunting opportunity is a process I have used to not only apply successfully to my own hunting endeavors since 1986, but to 100s of my client's hunting opportunities throughout a dozen states since 2005. I feel I have honed my craft into a defined set of concepts that you will learn if you follow along. I look forward to sharing my personal process of designing your own whitetail success. Also, make sure you read the conclusion of the book to find out what happened with that great 2011 encounter with one of MI's giants. There is a final surprise waiting for you that will assist you in understanding what it takes to experience success while designing your next great whitetail hunting experience.

09/20/11

Goals

Chapter 2

DESIGN GOALS

I assume since you are reading this book, that it is likely that your "deer focus" is similar to mine. What I mean by that is that any of us who have had the opportunity to work in the woods for whitetail deer share a similar set of goals. What I have enjoyed practicing in the whitetail woods, and what is a constant theme expressed by my clients, is to be able to do the following: Attract a quality deer herd (Attractability), Hold a quality deer herd during the hunting season (Holding ability), and effectively Hunt a quality herd (Huntability). Those goals may seem pretty basic, right? The problem is that while those goals may be universal, the path to achieving those goals is highly complex and will vary, literally, from neighboring property to neighboring property.

Too often the complexity of property design is fueled by the details of the multitude of habitat improvements or hunting styles that you may develop, or choose, for the lands you hunt. The perfect deer bed, the perfect food plot, the perfect tree, shrub, or type of grass...it never ends! On dozens of client parcels I have heard, "I was spending way too much time on the details." Basically, the art of "micro-managing" can be overwhelming because so much time can be spent within the details, while the actual results of those efforts can be limited or even counterproductive. In many walks of life success is indeed found within the details. However, I will make a case within the chapters of this book that the opposite can be said for a successful whitetail parcel, where the "death" of a parcel can be found within the details. You will experience success on your parcel when your improvements are located appropriately and work together to not only attract and hold a quality herd, but when they are located such that they allow you to access the lands you hunt without the deer you are hunting, know that you are hunting them.

Attractability

Bedding areas, food plots and even waterholes can be awesome sources of attraction...but while individually any of those improvements may be a very high priority on one parcel, it could be a very low priority on another. Part of the process of designing a whitetail parcel is diagnosing exactly what the deer need on your particular parcel. That can be a tough task in itself that I will discuss later, but once you figure out what you need, it's time to build your next great whitetail attraction. Building that attraction isn't the problem because there is an incredible amount of information available for planting beautiful fields of green, filling a bedding area full of cool looking deer beds, or installing a massive habitat planting of trees, shrubs and grasses. The problem instead lies in the fact that the more "attractive" you make an improvement, the higher the potential of spoiling the deer movement on your parcel. Let me explain...

Picture the scenario of a lush, green, high-powered patch of food within a 2-acre field on your hunting land. The local deer herd recognizes your food source as the #1 source for great dining within the entire neighborhood, and as the season draws near, deer from several parcels around, gravitate to your field of dreams. The table is set for a great deer season, right? Well, not

Water holes feature a high level of attraction but are also great places to hang a tree stand.

so fast. We need to back up a bit. Think about the attractions you are building for your parcel. Are you attracting a large number of deer to a certain area for food, cover, or water, only to send them scampering away when you enter or exit a deer stand, shut the car door prior to an afternoon sit, or while you open up your deer camp after a 3 hour drive from the city on a Friday night? One of the worst things we can do as deer hunters is to "lay a trap" of food, cover, or water…only to consistently spook those same deer away from that attraction. With that in mind, that 2-acre "perfect" food plot on your parcel may not be so perfect. With any attraction you are further ahead by not building that attraction in the first place if it means that you have to significantly increase the amount of times you run into, and subsequently "educate" deer, on your parcel.

The number of "Deer/Human Encounters" will destroy a property for the majority of the season. Part of your ultimate level of success is to continually make every attempt to lower those encounters. When you lay a trap that increases those encounters, your potential success goes down. However, when you lay a trap in a location that allows you to reduce your deer/human encounters, your success will go up. Using Paralleling Habitat Features, building Lines of Movement, and hunting with the skills of Predatory Access are all concepts that you can use to make sure the location and use of your improvements are working for you, and not against you. Attracting deer to your parcel is only one small piece of the puzzle that is often fairly easy to do, but getting those deer to stay on your property during the deer season is the hard part.

Holding Ability

Deer will gravitate to parcels that have no deer/human encounters in many cases even if the habitat is fairly poor. When late October rolls around, deer have often already been trained by hunters to key their movements relative to secure bedding and travel areas. However, when November rolls around in the Midwest, or as you enter the heart of the hunting season wherever you may be located, deer herds and in particular mature bucks, specifically seek out the most secure and "hunter free" daytime bedding areas. So the easy answer on your parcel is just to plain not hunt! Ok, I know that isn't going to be an option for any of you who are reading this book, or myself, but that's the goal. The goal is that you have to make the deer on your parcel think that they are not being hunted, while you hunt them. Making deer improvements to make it easier to hold deer, such as bedding areas and screening cover, are all great ways to enhance the holding ability of your parcel, but those improvements should not be made unless you can actually keep the deer within those daytime holding areas from knowing that you are actually hunting your parcel.

If you can attract and hold deer on your parcel during the months of the hunting season based on addressing the balance of food and cover needs on your parcel, then you can begin to plan for the hunt. But, can you have a great piece of habitat that both attracts and holds a whitetail herd while at the same time leaving you with a very difficult hunt? The answer is a definite YES!

Huntability

Your ability to move around the woods and be able to enter a high number of deer stands per acre safely, is the starting place for the most successful whitetail designs. Roads, adjoining habitat types, trail systems, and both food source and bedding area location possibilities, will determine what I call the "Framework" of your hunting design. The habitat types and features that fit within your framework are often aspects of your parcel that are difficult or impossible to change. How you fit your habitat improvements within the framework of your parcel will either make your hunting extremely easy, or extremely difficult. An extreme example of this would be a large, long narrow food source that points directly at your neighbor's parcel, ending within 20 yards of your property border. In that case a GREAT spot for your neighbor to sit would be about 40 yards back on his parcel as he hunts deer relating to an improvement that was built to clash within the framework of your parcel, instead of compliment it.

Attractability, Holding Ability, and Huntability

Those are some pretty broad goals that will be fully discussed in later chapters but I wanted to set the tone for the direction of this book through the large scale portion of planning the design of your whitetail hunting grounds. It's important that you start to think of your parcel, it's framework, and if your improvements, or potential improvements, are a good fit. Do your improvements compliment or clash with your framework? Are there improvements that you should possibly remove or change to make for a better fit and flow of your bedding areas, travel corridors, and food sources? Are there areas of your parcel where you have spent enormous amounts of man-hours perfecting the details, while your overall parcel design clashes with your framework? Again, one of the most common hindrances I see on most parcels, is in the "details"; meaning too much time spent on the details of habitat improvement, while ignoring the framework. Before making plans for your next great food plot or bedding area, take the time to analyze your major property components of roads, trails, habitat types, neighboring habitat types, high and low land, to see what kind of ultimate potential you have for your improvements, and keep asking yourself, "If I make this improvement, will I still be able to hunt my deer land without the deer knowing they are being hunted?"

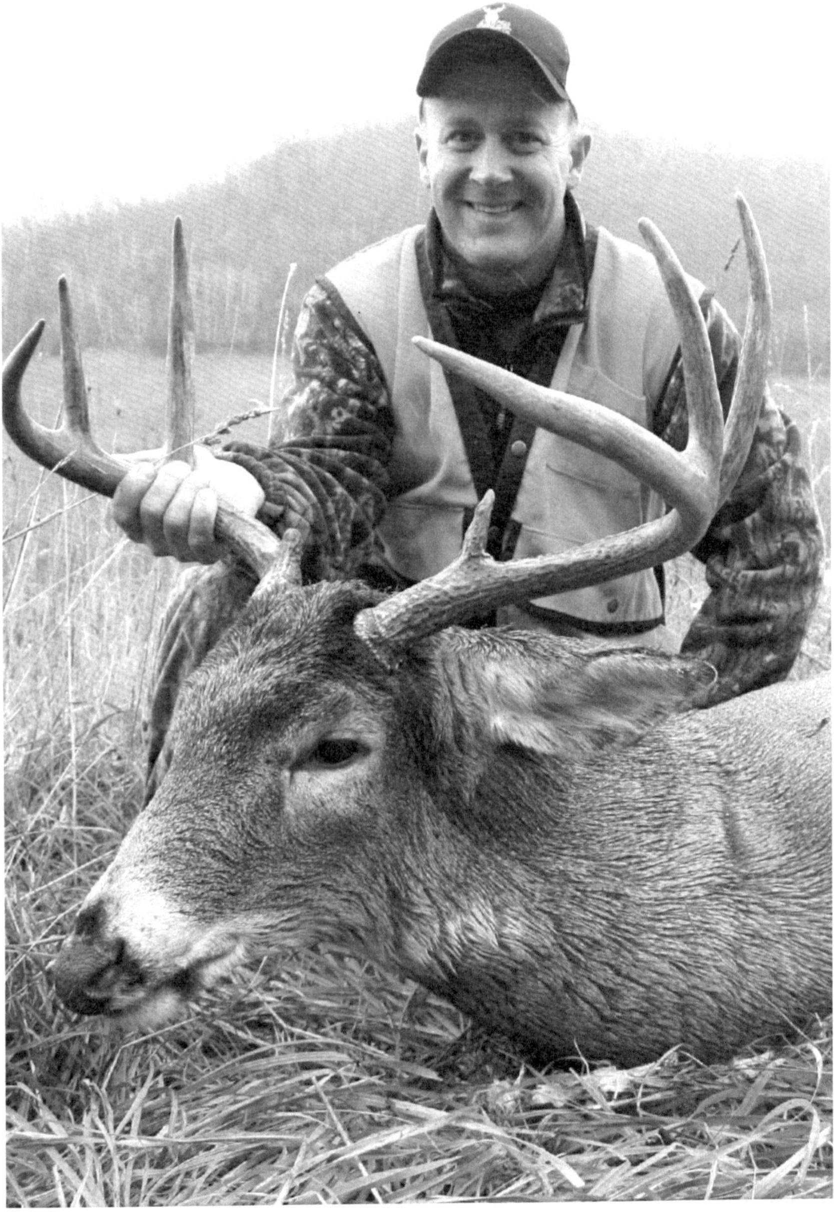

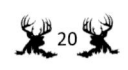

Structure

Chapter 3

ANALYZING THE FRAMEWORK OF YOUR HUNTING LAND

"Cookie Cutter Deer Movements"-- have you seen them? Various patterns involving both food and cover, habit planting designs, and even one that features a merry-go-round layout of deer movement where deer travel from food plot to food plot while hunters simply sit in a stand and watch deer basically spin like a top before their very eyes. Sounds cool, doesn't it? It would be, except for the fact that every piece of deer hunting land is so incredibly different! Every parcel is so different that I found that I could literally write a book on the subject. This book barely scratches the surface of habitat and hunting design. So for now, I'd like you to ignore cookie cutter deer movement designs, because while they may look cool on paper, they are often unrealistic in the real world.

Speaking of the real world, I realize that the many aspects of deer habitat and hunting design can be very overwhelming: deer beds, food plots, waterholes, neighbors, grass plantings, travel corridors, hinge-cuts, perennials, annuals, public land, private land, leased land, trespassers, seasoned hunters, new hunters, expectations, goals, hunter access, etc, etc, etc. To further complicate things, what do you need to discover within your own hunting grounds? What are you lacking? Sometimes it seems like hunting public land is easier; you simply define what you need for a successful hunt and go find it. With private land it often seems more difficult, because once you define what you need, you have to build it. Furthermore, defining what you need can be challenging. This is because your particular circumstances - in terms of access, elevation, and neighboring influences – may dictate that what you need is the complete opposite of what your neighbor needs. The only thing certain is that nothing is certain.

When clients first contact me, their heads are often swimming with ideas and thoughts. If I get too wrapped up with specific thoughts and ideas, we can be on the phone for hours. This can become highly unproductive if we spend too much time discussing specific details and not focusing on the more general concepts. My typical approach with a new client is to start with the framework of habitat design: where can you access your parcel? are there roads? what is your elevation? what is going on next door? My intention when speaking with a new client isn't to turn a four-hour conversation into five minutes. Rather, my goal is to get a pretty firm grasp of the three variables that I believe are critical to the potential design of the parcel: access, elevation, and neighboring influences. Once that framework is established, then everything else can fall into place. Follow along throughout this chapter and the rest of the book as I describe how those variables can be used effectively in a design that is unique to your hunting land.

Access

In my experience, I've found that 150 yards is the approximate distance that a deer can catch your scent through the woods. I say approximate, because it is impossible to account for all of the variables that enter into the equation. For example, for several years my lease partner and I used a stand on the north side of a steep hollow that had open air to the south for approximately 250 yards. We used the stand on the steep face while facing north, with a northerly wind. We actually had some good opportunities and sightings in this location, but the problem was that we learned, through personal observation while hunting a new stand to the south, that 250 yards was not enough open air to keep from blowing the deer out of one of our best bedding areas! Simply, one of us would use the north stand, the wind would blow into the bedding area 250 yards across the hollow, and we would watch deer exit the bedding area while we sat in the new stand to the south. I suspect that doe family groups may have tolerated our scent to some degree, but we were hurting our goal of holding mature bucks in the area. Once we stopped using that stand, we soon saw a drastic improvement in the amount of mature buck signs and harvested a

4 year old beauty that had taken a hunting season residence within the now "scentless" bedding area.

Most hunters probably consider whether a deer can see or hear you, but how often do you consider whether a deer can smell you as you access your stands? I have seen hundreds of "sanctuaries" in the form of small to large areas of land that hunters consider off limits to hunting and human use because they are attempting to offer a secure area to hold deer. For a sanctuary to be successful, it needs to be sound-free, sight-free, and scent-free. Take away one of those ingredients, and it's no longer a sanctuary. Deer may get used to the neighbor kids playing ball in the backyard, even if they can occasionally see the young superstars. But once one of the kids cross the line into their world, the game is over.

Deer can pattern hunters from their scent far better than we will ever have the ability to pattern them. To illustrate this point, imagine a 40-acre square parcel (440 by 440 yards) with an access trail that runs north to south through the middle of the parcel. If a hunter uses the trail during westerly winds, approximately 150 yards of cover on the east side of the entire trail will be saturated with scent. The same thing happens on the west side of the trail with easterly winds. With swirling winds, it's possible that ¾ of the entire parcel could be saturated with scent after just a few early season sits. Doe family groups may tolerate this central trail intrusion and may give the hunter the impression that everything is fine. For example, if you own an ATV, I suspect that you have seen a doe, fawn, or young buck stand motionless and watch you drive by on a trail. But how often has this happened with a mature buck? I have been using ATVs since the late 80s, and I have yet to witness my first mature buck drive-by.

I have found that you can use a deer's nose to your advantage. If deer move throughout your property in areas where they never pick up your sight, sound, or scent, and hunters move around the property with the wind in their favor, you can give the deer the illusion that everything is fine. Try to design access to your hunting stands so that the bulk of your land can be given to all deer all the time. Specifically, stand locations should be no further into the cover of your property than you care to potentially spook deer. This concept applies to public land too. One of the most important "secrets" I can reveal to you for public land scouting is to simply find the largest areas of public land that contain zero human scent, and then hunt those areas.

The more you restrict your travel and allow natural deer movements to take place without allowing your scent to enter the equation, the more you begin to dictate your own habitat and hunting design success. In the 40-acre parcel example, it may be possible to turn a scent-saturated 40-acre parcel into a 30-acre sanctuary where a deer never sees, hears, or smells you, by simply accessing only the exterior of the property. How many of your neighbor's property contains 30 or more acres of true sanctuary? It won't surprise me if your answer is zero, and that's why I believe that "access" is one of your most important hunting considerations in designing a hunting parcel.

Elevation

I love water! Swamps, creeks, rivers, ponds, and lakes can all offer incredible views, a variety of wildlife, and a great spot to blow your scent into when on a stand. Access to one of my favorite "fool-proof" deer stands involved walking across a 2-acre cemetery during the morning darkness (yes, pretty spooky even with a gun!), through a thick hedgerow, across 100 or so feet of flooded timber, and finally into a tree less than 5' from the water. A small expanse of field separated me from the river to the north, and I was never once busted by a deer either while I was traveling through the cemetery or the flooded timber. But let's look at this scenario a little differently. If the flooded timber was actually a swamp

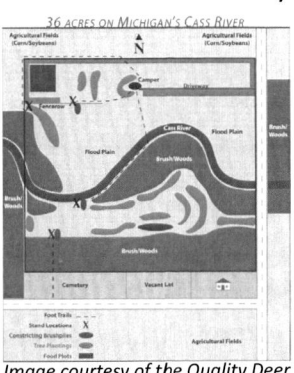

Image courtesy of the Quality Deer Management Association (QDMA)

with several feet of muck that was impossible to cross, then that "fool-proof" stand would now be impossible to hunt. No access, no hunting.

Something to consider when scouting your next hunting grounds is whether or not water exists on the property. Water can be a great addition to a hunting land, but don't proceed blindly just because a potential piece of hunting ground has a great water supply. Water can be efficiently added in the form of watering tanks or shallow ponds that avoid robbing large areas of habitat. Instead, consider how you can potentially access the land, and what that water source may be blocking off when considering the framework of your hunting design. Consider how you can use a larger open water source such as a pond or lake to capture your scent while on a stand, or even to navigate across to access stand locations adjacent to unsuspecting deer herds. Accessing stand locations by boat may be an incredible option for slipping in undetected to ambush a mature buck.

Another aspect to consider is how ridges and high elevation points affect your potential design. Ridges can be an outstanding way to access a stand undetected, and can also be used to hide many forms of habitat improvements. One of my favorite ways to get into a stand location is to start from the bottom of a ridge and walk up to the stand. By climbing into a tree stand from below the crest of the ridge, it may be possible to see the top of the ridge (and maybe even over the ridge) and view deer that haven't been exposed to your movements until literally the last few steps into the stand.

Dealing with high elevations can be as much of a challenge as low elevations, such as water. Discretely accessing a stand can be difficult if you have access via a high elevation point with the crest of the hill at your back, facing inward and down into your property. Unless you can offer thick screening cover, you are severely exposed under these conditions, and this has the potential to negatively affect your hunting efforts. Keep in mind that when accessing a stand location on your land involves walking in from above, your sight and sound can potentially carry a much greater distance.

Neighboring Influences

Planning to use neighboring influences – which may consist of roads, food sources, hunting pressure, or other human improvements (schools, factories, houses) – to HELP your hunting efforts, should occur at the beginning start of your property design, and not at the end. Over time, I have been able to develop some pretty solid "rules" of how to use neighboring influences to your advantage.

Roads

Hunters often shy away from parcels bordering roads when looking for their next favorite hunting grounds. This is largely based on their belief that land needs to be more secluded to harvest a mature buck. Growing up in southern Michigan's Oakland County (just north of Detroit), home to millions of people, I have seen giant bucks killed every year while attempting to cross the road in front of those millions of people. This has led me to form a different opinion about roads. Use them to your advantage!

> *Deer can become completely accustomed to human noise, scent, and movement along roads and highways. As long as those "road deer" don't see you, smell you, or hear you entering their world along the highway, they develop a very false sense of security.

> *Creating roadside bedding areas can be an outstanding tactic. While deer feel very comfortable bedding near the sights, sounds, and scents associated with a particular road, they do not typically cross that road. This is especially true when you offer the deer a high quality food source destination within your parcel.

*A road acts as a huge barrier between safety and threat. As long as you don't infringe into their area during the wrong time of the day or season, deer can become quite content.

*You can be efficient with your parcel design by locating your daytime bedding areas directly adjacent to the road border, while accessing stand locations through the road itself. In contrast, on parcels not bordered by roads, accessing stands from the perimeter of your parcel requires you to allocate a layer of your habitat to screening cover in addition to the width of your access trail. On a ¼-mile property line of a 40-acre parcel, every 33' of width devoted to your access equals a 1-acre reduction of available habitat. This loss of habitat can add up quickly when you consider all four sides of the property. For example, by using 100' of your 40-acre parcel for access trails and screening cover so that you can safely navigate the perimeter of your parcel without spooking deer, you have just lost over 10 acres of potential deer improvements. On the other hand, if your property has roads on two sides and you still want to access the remaining two sides, you lose only a little over 5 acres and have, therefore, gained over 5 acres for habitat improvements.

Bedding Areas

What do you do when your neighbor has the best bedding area in the county right along side the border of your parcel? You make sure that those deer feel extremely comfortable entering your parcel at anytime during the daytime hours.

*In my experience, offering a food plot next to a bedding area can result in housing deer on your neighbor's land, only to have them enter the food on your parcel after spending the majority of daytime hours somewhere else. If you spook the deer off the food source by attempting a risky food-side stand location, you may force those deer to stay on your neighbor's land until after dark and enter the food source after it's too late to hunt. Furthermore, mature bucks will rarely pass through the middle of a food source during daylight hours, so a food source located adjacent to a neighbor's bedding area has the potential to block a lot of movement onto your parcel.

* As described in Chapter 13, I have experienced that doe family groups will often bed within the first available bedding cover adjacent to a food source, and bucks will tend to bed behind the does, farther away from the food source. This concept can be used to address the situation of a high-quality bedding area on a neighboring property. Specifically, you can offer a secure sanctuary on your land, adjacent to the neighbor's bedding cover. In addition, give the deer a reason to travel across the entire length of your property, to access a major food source. If you can accomplish this, then deer will feel comfortable moving freely from your neighbors high quality bedding area, throughout your sanctuary and ideally to the food source on your property. You can attempt to house doe family groups closest to the food source, and then still have room to house immature and mature bucks within the remaining cover extending to the sanctuary on your parcel border. I am not sure that the concept of doe family groups and bucks having layered bedding locations applies everywhere a whitetail roams, but I have experienced it enough to consistently enjoy the success when the practice is employed.

*Even if your neighbor has the highest quality bedding area in the county, I have found that these bedding areas can be a ghost town during daytime hunting hours if they lack the compliment of food. Specifically, deer prefer locations that offer hunting season forages and adequate daytime bedding opportunity over high-quality bedding areas with no nearby food. When you offer secure bedding areas on your own land with no human intrusion, it won't take the local deer herd long to recognize that they are just a few bounds away from secure bedding on your parcel if they are pushed off your neighbor's property due to sloppy hunting. This holds true even if the bedding habitat on your property is of lower quality. A secure and adequate bedding area trumps an un-secure, high-quality bedding area. Understanding this is a great way to use your neighbor's high-quality bedding area to your own advantage, even if you can't offer the same level of quality on your own land.

Food Sources

Neighboring food sources can be an outstanding tool to your overall habitat and hunting design strategy, because they allow you to devote less land to food sources and more land to daytime cover. In addition, it has been my experience that harvesting a mature buck over a food source can be difficult. Consequently, if a neighboring food source is being hunted frequently, it doesn't take many careless intrusions for those deer to start spending their daylight hours within the cover on your land, instead of your neighbors.

*A great way to use a neighboring food source to your advantage is to plant a little food on your land where the deer can feed before they exit your property to find larger and greener pastures after dark. Similarly, establishing several mock scrapes or even water if it is lacking in the area, increases the possibility that deer will stay on your property closer to dark before entering your neighbor's food sources to feed into the night.

*Offering a much higher level of security on your parcel than your neighbors by minimizing human intrusion and hunting pressure, can be a huge advantage as well. It's critical to keep the bulk of your parcel "safe" for deer, so that the deer in the area recognize the difference between your parcel and your neighbor's. When this is accomplished, expect the local deer herd to be on your parcel the majority of legal shooting light, and not on your neighbor's.

*A large, high-quality food source on neighboring property can work to your advantage, particularly if the neighbor's property has little bedding cover or lacks enough depth to house both doe family groups adjacent to the food source and bucks behind. I see this situation on a lot of parcels that are "food plot crazy", meaning that the vast majority of their parcel is either food plots, agricultural land, or both. Under these conditions, there isn't enough cover necessary to support those food sources. And where do those deer turn when that happens? On to your land...if you plan for it!

Hunting Pressure

I love when there is a certain degree of hunting pressure on lands adjacent to where I hunt. When most people think of hunting pressure, they think of loud, obnoxious, and unrelenting human intrusion that borders on trespassing. This can be a very good thing because you can easily plan for loud and obnoxious. What you can't plan for is quiet and strategic because those type of hunters (hopefully like yourself) never really show you, or the deer, what they are up to, how they hunt, and where they will turn up next.

*Neighbors who hunt quietly and strategically are typically of little concern to most hunters. In reality, those are often the hunters who are shooting mature bucks. Furthermore, those are also the hunters who typically don't even tell you what they are shooting. In contrast, loud and obnoxious hunters...well, that's a good thing! One of my favorite neighboring groups in WI starts the opener of gun season by turning the key on their ATVs. Even though they do it only a handful of times a year, deer vacate their property before they even turn off the hard-top road and start traversing through their open fields. We have witnessed dozens of deer exit their parcel with just the turn of a key. It's not surprising that we are very thankful those neighbors would rather ride than walk.

*By offering secure bedding and transitional cover adjacent to obnoxious hunting pressure, it is very easy to collect deer on your property as the hunting season progresses and pressure increases. A good strategy is to look for ways to improve the habitat adjacent to neighboring high-pressure areas and then incorporate those features within the overall framework of your habitat and hunting design. By creating the opportunity for deer to escape, seek shelter, and hide on your property, it is possible that the number of mature buck sightings – or deer sightings in general – can increase on your property as the season progresses.

*High-pressure parcel borders can be an outstanding spot from which to access your parcel. Deer become accustomed to the sights, sounds, and scents of human intrusion along a high-pressure border, so use these situations to your advantage. You may find it easy to slip into stand locations just inside your borders, to ambush deer that have been lulled into a false sense of security by the relative lack of hunting pressure just across the fence line.

Human Improvements

Schools, factories, churches, houses, cabins, and other human improvements are the ultimate dead-end of deer movement and are GREAT locations for food sources on your property. In fact, it may be possible to offer a well-screened and hidden dead-end food source behind your hunting cabin. Once a deer reaches the destination of food within your borders, that deer often has no place to go but back into the heart of your parcel.

*By offering a dead-end food source just inside your habitat, near human improvements, you can contain deer within bedding cover near the opposite end of your parcel and draw deer to the hidden food source every evening. Those lines of movement can be long, continuous, consistent, and easy to hunt as deer transition from bedding cover to food source and back to bedding cover every day.

*If your parcel is long and narrow with a human improvement on one end, you can effectively house deer in many layers of bedding cover throughout the entire length of your parcel. This concept – referred to as Depth of Cover, and explained in detail in Chapter 6, offers the possibility of deer transitioning back and forth from a dead-end food source on one end of your property to bedding areas on the other.

*Don't be distraught if your next great piece of hunting land seems spoiled because it is located adjacent to a school, factory, church, house, or cabin. Instead, enjoy the positives and learn to take advantage of what your neighbors are offering. Having areas that the deer are NOT using is often just as important – or maybe even more important – than having areas that the deer ARE using.

Conclusion

In a short time a fertile piece of agricultural land can be turned into a brush-choked sanctuary full of daytime bedding whitetails, mature hardwoods can be turned into thousands of pounds per acre of fresh woody browse and security cover, and an infertile field of bracken fern can be turned into a lush, green food plot. However, Access, Elevation, and Neighboring Influences are all features of habitat design that are almost impossible to change to any large degree. By focusing first on what CAN NOT be changed instead of what CAN be changed, you will be well on your way to establishing the framework of an outstanding hunting and habitat design. Over the years I have learned to steer the conversation with potential clients to those three basic talking points to begin establishing the initial framework of their parcel. Those three points alone will help establish a multitude of habitat improvement possibilities before ever gassing up a chainsaw or turning the crank on a hand spreader. Although "Cookie Cutter Deer Movements" may work extremely well on paper, the variables that influence the design of your next deer hunting opportunity dictate a flexibility that can make the mind swim with possibilities. Instead of focusing on the multitude of mind-swimming variables, focus on three things – Access, Elevation, and Neighboring Influences – so that the odds can be tilted much more in your favor.

Chapter 4
ROAD KILL MAP TO HABITAT SUCCESS

Maybe it's because I've splattered 6 deer across the grill of my pickup...ok well, 5 on my pickup and 1 on my ex-wife's new Suburban with less than 500 miles...but over the years I've learned to take a keen eye to potential deer crossings. Of course, when you are traveling at 60+ and smack a deer, you tend to take notice after the screeching tires, sound of broken parts, and sudden stop. I remember a few years ago a friend's ankle hurt for a week after slamming on the brake, ON THE PASSANGER side of the vehicle, as I was driving and ran into a deer. Without a doubt the exact location, sound, and feel of that "Road Kill Experience" is burned into her memory. But let's take this one step further. Have you ever looked at a road kill, and thought, "why in the heck did that deer cross the road, at that spot?" Have you ever looked out across the landscape to connect the dots? And for that matter, what time of day or night those deer may have been crossing? I have personally found that deer simply don't just cross the road to get to the other side.

When deer move they typically do it for a very specific reason, and in a very particular travel pattern. Sure, the name "Road Kill" actually sounds kind of humorous, but in all seriousness, for those of us who travel a lot, even for a living, I think it stands to reason that we can learn a lot about deer behavior, hunting, and even how to design our own deer habitats, if we just take a little bit more notice of our nation's ever plentiful road kills. I remember a while back that in MI alone there were 55,000 reported deer road kills. To me, that's 55,000 opportunities to become better educated about deer movements, hunting, and design opportunities. And let's face it; learning about deer has a lot to do with deer/human encounters. Some complain they go an entire season and see 30 deer or less, but on a trip from the Mackinaw Bridge in Northern MI to the Detroit area, it's hard NOT to see at least 30 dead deer in one trip. When you think about it, that's a lot of potential learning ripening along the road!

Follow along with me and I'm going to discuss how these deer crossing observations will help you learn a little more about deer behavior, deer hunting, and ultimately how to apply it to the successful design of your next whitetail hunting endeavor.

Behavior by Road Kill

You've heard it before, but deer are creatures of "Edge". What's an edge? In deer behavior I'd like to describe an edge as a tree line, fencerow, type of habit change, age of habitat change, ditch, ridgeline, waterline...make sense? Even the edge of the road, is an "edge." When you travel down the highway, look several hundred yards ahead and see those edges all coming together. When you see a field edge, timberline, ditch, and change in topography all coming together to form a very defined line running right at the road...watch out! At the same time look for reinforcement in those areas in the form of rubs and previous road kills. There is a spot south of Roscommon, MI, on I-75, where there is a HUGE marsh on both sides of the road that carries enough water to be one giant bumper of deer movement activity. As you travel northbound you can look on the east side of the road as you approach the north end of the marsh. As the Marsh transitions into scattered small jack pine followed by an eventual stand of mature pines, it's hard not to notice the pronounced rub line running right at the highway. No, I haven't seen a deer cross the road in this location, let alone a buck, but it speaks volumes for deer behavior and what you should be looking for when scouting vast open public lands for hunting. You don't even have to leave the highway and you can already narrow down thousands of acres spanning on both sides of the highway, to begin searching for a stand location starting with 1 single rub line. Find the edge, and deer will be following it as evidenced by both deer crossing signs and road kills.

A parcel of private land I owned in the past often featured a rub line that crossed the county road that traveled through my property. I worried that hunters would notice the rub line, and then relate that to ariel photos that would help them identify potential stand locations within the adjacent National Forest. My answer? I cut the trees down on my own land that featured the rubs within site of the road, and eliminated a potential clue into the unraveling of mature buck movements within the area. A drastic step? Maybe. However, as someone who is constantly intrigued by mature buck movements and the clues those old monarchs leave, it was an obvious roadside strategy.

One of the things you may notice is a dead deer without an edge connecting to the road, and with very little "safe" cover approaching the road. What does this tell you? That this is a nighttime crossing. At the same time, while looking across the field, there is often an edge pointing like a giant arrow right at the road...a swale, a point of woods, fencerow...it just doesn't extend to the road itself. Even if that edge is ¼ mile away, you may be able to see the culprit, to the demise of that particular deer.

Suburban crossings are classic too...large subdivision on the right, large woods on the left, and as you travel ahead you notice a deer crossing sign. Is it any wonder why the deer crossing sign is located at the line of woods that crosses the road in front of you from behind the subdivision? I recently saw a "Letter to the Editor" in a local newspaper urging county officials to "Please move the deer crossing sign because it is in a busy location, and it would be better if the deer crossed in a location that would be safer for deer and driver." Of course, deer were crossing there because the sign told them to, right? Ummm, sure! Instead, the subdivision acted as one giant bumper of deer activity no different than a huge marsh, lake, or even to some extent the large open-understory of a "sometimes deer less" mature stand of hardwoods.

Hunting by Road kill

You have to ask yourself, "Why did that deer attempt to cross in this location"? It's not too difficult to remember those crossings, and to go back home to reference an ariel photo of the area. Notice the edges, connect the dots, and then apply it to your hunting. If you pay attention while on the road you will find that the puzzle of edge and deer behavior becomes very predictable and definitive. File all those dead "deer encounters" within your memory bank and take it to your whitetail woods. This is probably why I love to hunt large open marshes or thousands of acres of similar habitat. Subtle changes in topography or habitat become very noticeable from the air or on the ground; and if you can find where those edges form an "X" or "T" within the woods, you can find some pretty deadly stand locations. Better yet, the longer and stronger the edge, the easier it is to position stand locations for various wind and hunter approach patterns.

What is pretty cool is that even though you can travel thousands of miles through different whitetail habitats, and even though the types of habitats drastically change, deer will still follow those various forms of edges no matter what state you might be hunting in. It's not so much the type of habitat...just the change. In that way it's not too hard to look at an ariel photo of a 10,000 acre tract of public land, and narrow it down to less than 100 acres of "X"s and "T"s to scout for hunting, all while applying those lessons learned when paying attention to a bunch of rotting deer carcasses along the road.

Designing by Roadkill

Sure, it's simple, right? Put a bunch of edges on your property to hunt, throw up a stand...and shoot something. In part, that's correct. However, the problem comes when you point those edges right off your property! Think of those edges as one big giant arrow of deer movement. Point the arrow OFF of your property...and the deer will follow. So, while it is critical to use edge creation on your own parcel to create definitive deer movement, whether that be by creating deer travel corridors, long food sources, timber cuttings, or habitat changes, it's also just as critical to turn that edge BACK onto your property to continue the deer movement within the confines of your own property border. Point an arrow off of your parcel and you can't get too upset when your neighbor places a stand right where the arrow is pointing, only 20 yards into his own parcel. In other terms, if your hunting land is located along a highway and you place a 200 yard long x 20 yard food plot running straight to within 20 yards of that highway...would you really be that surprised if that giant 6 year old you've been after gets smacked on the road? You shouldn't be. You quite possibly pushed him to his death no differently than running that same buck on an arrow you created, right at your neighbor's deer stand.

Conclusion

Road kill edges can convey a powerful message of deer behavior, potential hunting success, and whitetail habitat design. The great thing is, you can learn about all 3 from the comfort of your hunting pickup with the cruise set at 72, jamming to some tunes, and with a few hunting buddies swapping deer stories. Better yet, you can take the time to explain these things to your kids in the car; and those future hunters can learn a TON about deer, deer hunting, and deer habitat without ever stepping foot into the woods. Again ,"Road kill" does sound kind of humorous, but I hope you can see the value in paying just a little more attention to deer crossings...whether you run into them with your wife's brand new Suburban, or not.

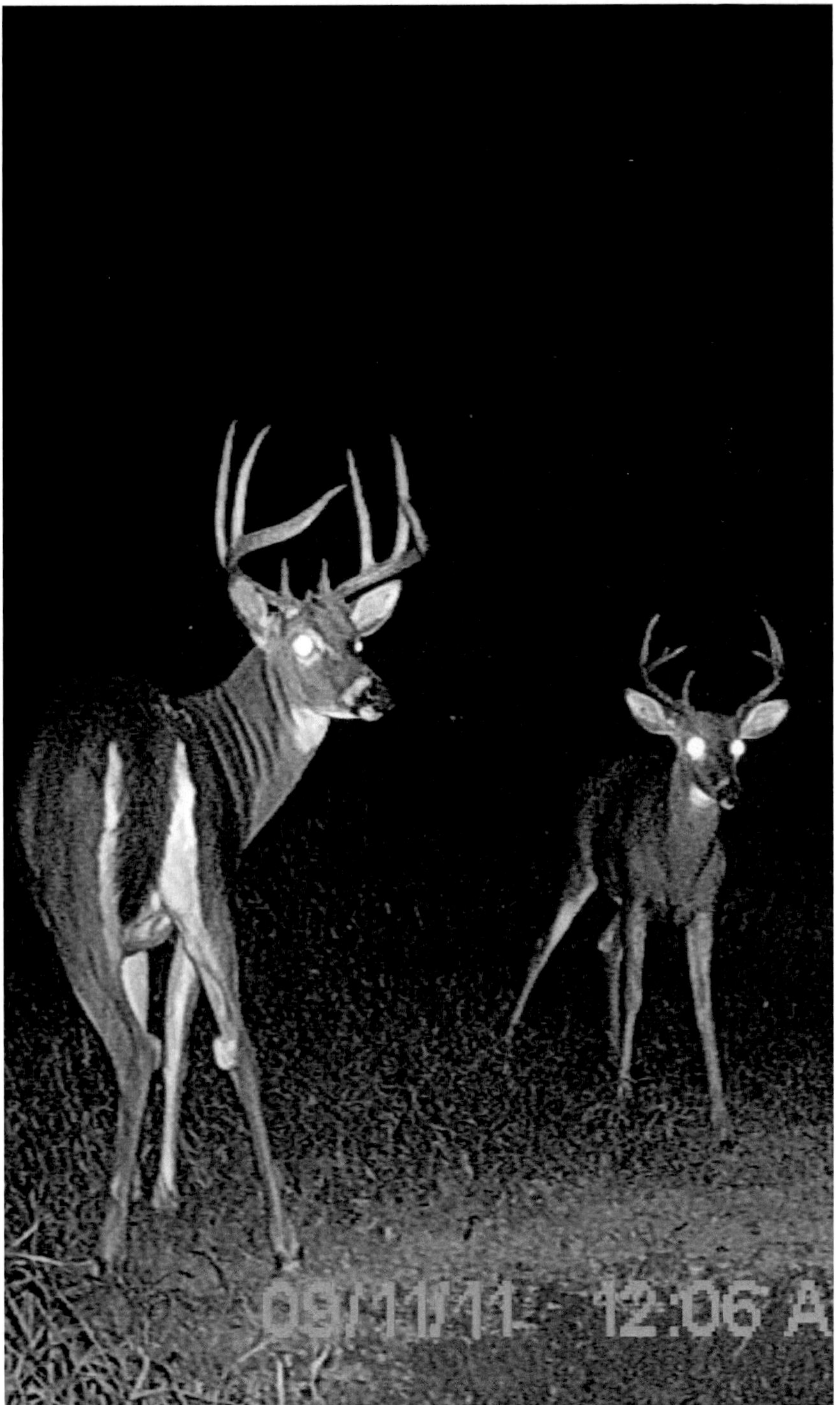
09/11/11 12:06 A

Chapter 5

HIDE AND SEEK HABITAT CHANGES

How many of you liked the childhood game of "Hide and Seek?" I did! And I remember when I played, that I not only liked to be the last one found, I liked to be the one that couldn't be found in the first round, 2nd, 3rd, 4th, and until after the game was over. In fact, the best was hiding until everyone was finished looking and were just about to give up. I would finally have to reveal my spot that was often right under their nose. The dirty back corner of a garage, under a shelf behind a couple of old pallets…. maybe inside a pile of leaves against a chain-link fence, basically out in the open…. or possibly the upper shelf of a closet behind a single row of shoeboxes while the other boxes were placed neatly under the bed. The point was to hide within as many changes in structure as possible. The changes in structure were essentially any form of change that caused the seeker to possibly give up. For example, a closet door, an upper shelf, a row of boxes, a fence, a pile of leaves, a tuft of weeds, or a few shelves, a back corner, and a couple of old pallets. Most people stop after the first change or two, and the person hiding then, of course, stays hidden. Also, once the hiding spot is ½ searched, the seeker usually doesn't come back for another investigation, and if they do…those additional changes make the spot even better.

I've often found that deer in general, especially a reclusive, old, low-stress seeking monarch, tends to choose a daytime hiding spot relative to the many changes of habitat that exist in nature. Similar to all of those "structure" changes that created a great hiding spot while playing "Hide and Seek" as a youngster, "habitat" changes work just the same. Ridges, benches, mature timber, young timber, changes in timber type, seasonal habitat changes, rivers, swamps, fields, food sources, etc. are just a few of the habitat changes that you may find on your own hunting grounds. By focusing on the changes in habitat when choosing where, when, and how to hunt, whether it be on public, private, or leased lands, you are on the path to experience the ultimate in whitetail success. In order to understand where a deer is hiding, or where you can get him to hide, you have to first understand the use of habitat changes in your whitetail deer pursuits.

Where to Hunt

Obviously, if you have your own little slice of heaven, then you hopefully will be developing a cohesive implementation and usage of many habitat changes to improve your overall experience. Timber cuttings, habitat plantings, food source development, water sources, and bedding area enhancement practices, are all at your disposal to attain the "perfect" plan on your parcel relative to your individual parcel needs. If you don't have it and it will fit within your plan...get it! When you develop a plan, though, you not only offer a safe spot for the local deer herd to call home, but if you define that location enough, you have a great opportunity to sneak in for the kill. Best of all, on private land, you can take many years to perfect your plan by fine tuning, making adjustments, and learning "on the go." On public land, though, searching for those habitat changes and then making some sense of those changes to predict travel, bedding, and feeding patterns, becomes the name of the game, albeit a much faster-paced game than building it yourself, on your own land.

In the northern public lands of MI's Upper Peninsula, the habitat can be continuous and almost boring. However, that is a very good thing because there is nothing better than using habitat change to take a 10,000 acre wilderness tract of public land and narrow it down to less than 100 acres of potential hunting locations. You can avoid continuous hardwoods, ignore the impenetrable tag alder swamps, and not be tempted to follow that marsh-cut deer trail that travels for over a mile across a vast wetland of open grasses and occasional spruce clumps. Instead, draw a red circle around where that hardwood ridge, tag alder swamp, and marsh all meet, possibly on a long point of funneled deer usage. Put an "X" over the areas within ½ mile of any road or trail, place a star over the areas with a beaver damn or water source to potentially cause the careless to get a little wet...and you've just eliminated 99% of the entire area that you can just simply ignore. Scan ariel photos and topographical maps first, before spending about a ½ day searching, for areas that feature the most adjoining habitat changes in one spot as determined by those photos and maps, and you will most likely experience success. Draw up a plan of attack to have multiple stand locations for varying wind and weather patterns, 2 different ways to access the location, and have fun!

In the rolling public land hardwoods of northern PA, I found a great pattern of habitat changes that included the highest elevation line of a hemlock bottom, a hidden bench, a south facing ridge of new growth, and a stream edge. By sitting on the downwind side in a pre-positioned climbing stand adjacent to the location featuring the highest concentration of large rubs, and using the deeply cut stream as a hidden and scent-free access, the table was set for a great sit for a mature buck! I can think of at least one 30 square mile area fitting the above description that you could basically narrow down to about 7 separate possible locations to scout within a few hours on a Sunday afternoon prior to the Monday opener of PA's rifle season. Your scouting area may only include 20 acres of total acreage minus the travel in-between. That pattern of habitat is extremely common throughout the region, and by focusing on habitat change to define your hunting efforts wherever you hunt, you can design a high level of whitetail success.

When to Hunt

The best example of habitat change I can think of that relates to "When" to hunt, is the case of an 80-acre stand of mature hardwoods adjacent to a rich agricultural region. Acorns dropping, trees in their spectacular fall foliage, a few well-placed water holes, and adjacent succulent summer-range food sources, all equal a high % of early season success. However, remove those crops, drop the foliage, dry up or freeze the waterholes, and vacuum up the acorns with a few dozen turkeys and a small herd of deer, and it's often hard to find a deer track during late November. Try using the seasonal change in habitat patterns to determine the optimum time to hunt. On public land this may mean seeking stands of conifer adjacent to food sources during the late season, and on private land this may mean adding those food sources or conifer stands of snow-hindrance and thermal protection to build a late season deer herd on your property. If you pay attention to the seasonal patterns of habitat change, you can enjoy hunting the right place at the right time on the lands you typically hunt, even if you have to plan on another place to hunt during the wrong times.

How to Hunt

Nothing spoils a great spot, a spot where many types of habitat change come together to produce a logical pattern of travel, feeding, or bedding...than by accessing that spot at the wrong time, or in the wrong stand location. By using a downwind side, by focusing on "deer free" approaches, and by staying OUT of the hub of deer usage and activity you can not only experience a great sit with a low % of possible deer/human disturbance, but you can preserve that spot for another day. On public land that may mean that you simply enjoy the entire day out in the woods and then leave after a few days while dreaming of next year. However, on private lands, the concept becomes much more critical to preserve. Think of your private hunting grounds as having the ability to age like a fine wine. As your neighbor's are potentially spoiling their parcels with poor hunting efforts, the local deer herd will easily distinguish the "safety" and security of your non-invasive tactics used to maximize the effectiveness of the many habitat changes that you have taken the time to create. After you assemble those habitat changes in a logical pattern of movement across the entire landscape, as discussed in later chapters, those un-interrupted manipulations of deer movement will become stronger every day, making the deer increasingly easier to ambush when the time is right.

In the market to buy or lease?

By seeking out parcels with as many habitat changes as possible, you will be years ahead of the game because large-scale habitat changes don't take place quickly. Then, after finding a diverse piece of land, it's just a matter of stepping in and enhancing the appropriate locations that fit within the best pattern of potential movement and deer usage for your parcel. You can even add some quick habitat changes to the plan, if appropriate, to strengthen the intended pattern of manipulation for example, through timber harvest or native grass plantings. Also, by NOT enhancing the areas that fall outside of the intended overall plan, those areas become quickly distanced in both overall quality and deer usage, making it easier for you to move about your new property purchase or lease without spooking the deer that "you" are hiding on your parcel.

Conclusion

Can memories of a child-hood game hold one of the keys to your whitetail success? I think so! I'm not suggesting pallets or head-high piles of leaves within your favorite hunting land. But come to think of it, I'd rather have open hardwoods with a few long rows of head-high leaves to add some habitat change and possibly increase the level of security the deer feel in an otherwise boring woodlot. Give the local deer herd a place to hide within a logical web of habitat changes, and in turn give yourself a chance to locate a hidden buck of a lifetime, a buck that unwittingly hid within YOUR favorite hiding spot!

Above: 2011 UP of Michigan Public Land Below: 2009 PA Public Land

Chapter 6

DEFINE AND CONQUER

A 2007 client of mine contacted me with a problem he was having on a particularly large parcel of land...at least large when it comes to a typical Midwestern ag-land hunting parcel. While my average client has approximately 80 acres - 20 to 40 is pretty common, this client had over 500 acres of contiguous draws, springs, ridges, hidden benches, hardwoods, and enough hidey-holes to house a small army of mature bucks. So what was my client's dilemma? His neighbor with 30 acres was shooting the largest and most mature bucks within the area. Now many of you won't feel sorry for my client, we'll call him "Ed", because he was still consistently harvesting 3 and 4-year old bucks scoring in the 140-150 class. However, it was those 5 year olds and older that he was really after, and with the type of investment he had into his hunting property, I could understand why!

Part of why I enjoy visiting a client parcel is to diagnose that parcel, and Ed had an overwhelming problem in stand placement because they were all in the "middle-range". What I mean by "middle range" stand locations is that they were too far into the cover for the needed doe harvest, but not quite far enough to take advantage of the many hidden benches and stream crossings that the mature boys were using to parallel the edges of the ag land. What I often find is that the larger the parcel size, the harder it is to pinpoint stand locations in order to shoot the mature bucks every year, simply because

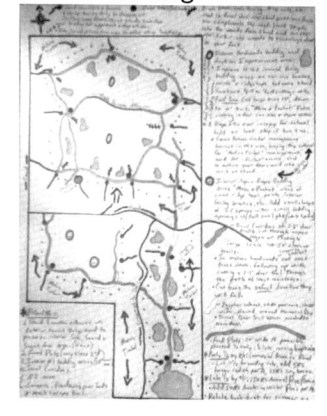

Defining stand location for client parcels starts first by defining habitat improvements

there are too many options. A "dream" parcel can actually be too overwhelming to the point that it becomes confusing and almost too difficult to master. On the other hand, a parcel size of 40 acres offers the landowner fewer options for stand placement, access, bedding area construction, food source location, and overall layout and design. The landowner can "master" his parcel and understand every square inch of habitat and topography because of the small size. Also, I believe although a mistake or two on a small parcel is certainly more magnified, it's easier to avoid them. Regardless of my beliefs, though, the point of this article is to illustrate the fact that on a small parcel it is much easier to specifically define the deer usage and movements. On a large parcel the temptation is to take such a micro-management approach that there is no flow or continuity of deer movement. When there is no flow to a parcel, that parcel can become very difficult to manage.

So how do you make sure the flow of your parcel is optimum? It has been my experience that the overall size of the improvements, the location of the improvements, and the continuity of the improvements need to be within a very precise design, whether the parcel contains many acres, or just a few.

Size-Don't Overdo it!

Yes, too much of a good thing is just that, too much! Even on a 40-acre parcel it pays to intensely design the bedding areas and food sources just enough to specifically dictate where the local deer herd will be. I hear often about making a small parcel as full of improvements as possible...especially when it comes to bedding area and cover-"improving every square inch." However, how many deer do you really want to hold?

Although I don't advocate it, I've witnessed 20 deer living the bulk of their lives within 5 acres of high-quality cover. In my experience it's not about improving the entire 40 acres; it's about defining those improvements within an adequate enough size to accomplish your herd management goals, but not so large as to detract from your ability to access and effectively harvest the deer of your choice throughout the entire hunting season.

I often get the question of how my recommendations may differ from that of a forester. Well, for one, if you have me coming out, I would venture a guess that your priority is more about deer, and less about timber. On a 500 acre parcel of hardwood a forester may establish a 60-year rotational cutting so that every 5 years 50 acres is cut, resulting, in theory, that the entire parcel will be completely cut every 60 years, continuing on a never ending harvest of rotational timber cuttings. If your goal is to build a quality deer herd and to be able to hunt that herd, consistently taking both an adequate amount of does, AND the most mature of the bucks that reside in and around the property, then a rotational timber harvest practice may be contrary to your goals. The reason? You will always be playing "catch up," basically letting the deer make you react to their continually changing movements, as a result of the ever changing food sources and cover locations that will be created by the continued cuttings. Instead, it's a much better practice to specifically install the appropriate bedding area space, as well as food source locations and access so that YOU as the land manager dictate what the deer do, and so that YOU, the land manager, has the ultimate level of control over your success. Through timber management you have an incredible opportunity to offer diversity in both age and quality. For example, for your access and areas downwind of stand locations...basically "deer-free" zones, you may have the opportunity to offer areas for old-growth timber management. I like a timber management plan for a parcel of hardwoods that would include old growth timber management in access and downwind blocking areas, portions of select cut for optimum timber management, and areas of clear-cutting within designated and unchanging bedding areas. The bulk of valuable hardwood forests can and should be still managed for optimum value and future "boards per foot," but the framework and overall design of your property can be defined first.

The bedding areas, food sources, access points, and stand locations need to be precise, and actively managed for the foreseeable future, and from what I have seen, should rarely change unless various factors of exterior property influence and/or experience within your parcel dictate. And for those components to be precise, they need to be defined. Small and defined, is better than large and random. Bedding areas effectively screened and correctly installed so as to separate and segregate the local deer population within a logical pattern relating to your food sources and travel corridors, is a great start to your design. And it should be the same with your food sources; meaning, just enough to offer what your parcel needs without being so large that they inhibit your ability to move throughout the parcel quietly and non-invasively.

Location of the Improvements

As discussed earlier, not only should the locations of the improvements not change, they should be actively maintained and managed for the foreseeable future, unless conditions arise that dictate change. Personally, I've had to remove a few food plots throughout the years, not due to quality or productivity, but instead due to the fact that they were simply in the wrong location…great improvements, wrong spot! Too many times a location is defined by convenience, soil type, or tradition. Instead, a location should be defined because that location fits within a logical pattern of cohesive deer usage and movement within your property's boundaries.

What are some of the aspects of location to consider? The main factor would probably be, "does this improvement give you, as the hunter and landowner, the ability to move around and into your parcel without spooking game". A bedding area that gets too close to your parcel boundary so that you can't walk around your parcel, a food plot that gets too close to your hunting movements, or even a travel corridor that brings the deer too close to your hunting scent or sound, should all be avoided. If it takes being smaller to be hidden, then by all means shrink the improvement. Also, how does this improvement relate to the other improvements on your parcel? As in the case of the large 500-acre parcel, are any of the improvements a "dead end"? Often many of the improvements should act to facilitate deer movement and continual usage within the confines of your parcel. A "dead-end" improvement forces the deer to make a choice...to leave within an undefined pattern of movement, possibly on the way to your neighbors, or just as bad, into your actual movements as you are attempting to move throughout the parcel without spooking game. In some cases a dead-end food source adjacent to a large human development can be a great strategy, but I will discuss that concept in a later chapter. Much of the time with the location of the improvement, it all boils down to keeping your deer/human encounters to as low a % as possible.

Continuity of Improvements

By now I hope you have a clear picture that your property improvements need to "flow" for you to be able to achieve a high degree of whitetail success. A smooth transition from bedding, to feeding, to travel corridors, and back and forth, means a lower stress level within the entire local herd. The reason I believe this, is because the more you can come close to encompassing a deer's daily travel patterns, the more of a chance those movements can be defined enough to avoid your movements as a hunter. Maybe it can be looked at in a different way, but to me, lower deer/human encounters = lower stress levels for the local deer herd. Deer can travel, move, and go back again without exposing themselves to neighboring influences, as well as the influences of your own movements. When continuity of a low-stress daily movement takes place, it is a work of beauty! By offering adequate bedding cover and food sources throughout the months of the hunting season, together with the established continuity of stress-free movements and daily patterns, you will typically increase the deer numbers on your parcel the later the hunting season progresses. And although initially a higher deer population might make you think the deer numbers could be too high; think again. In my experience, the higher numbers are not from the more tolerant doe herd that will typically stick within their preferred fall hangouts, despite the increased hunting pressure. Instead, I find that on my parcel the buck population is what is doubling or tripling as the season progresses, as hunter-wary mature bucks seek a more stable environment of seclusion and safety. Now THAT is a thing of beauty.

Conclusion

It's not about how much you can improve your parcel, but instead how those improvements can be defined and fit together. It's better to work slowly to define and fit together the pieces within the appropriate framework of movement and design on your parcel as a work in progress for a few years, than to fall into the temptation of doing too much too quickly without fully understanding the intricacies of your parcel and local deer herd movements. You may be familiar with the concept of trying to make a small parcel seem larger through diversity. Well, often it's not a bad idea to make a large parcel seem smaller through specifically defining the pieces of a logical puzzle together on a larger scale, and then filling in the gaps of improvement through experience, time, or both. Attack your parcel through precision and continuity, and then conquer your hunting and management goals through a definitive flow while remembering that too much of a good thing is just that...too much!

Chapter 7
DEPTH OF COVER

How many of you enjoyed mathematics as your favorite subject in school? I have to admit that while math and writing were my "easiest" subjects, there was only one of those two that captured my heart and mind, and it wasn't math. I can still remember attempting long, tedious Advanced Algebra calculations as "Mr. Brown" would forever remind my classmates and me of how much we would later use math in the real world. Whether that statement is true or not for you today, most likely is determined by your choice of career. What is personally interesting is that while writing is a huge part of my career, I still haven't been able to shake my "passion" for math. It is forever burned into my brain that an acre is 43,560 Sq.Ft. Parcel sizes, food plot acreages, woodlot sizes, seed, fertilizer, lime and chemical amounts, are some of the basic formulas...and I won't even pretend to be schooled in the calculations of boards per foot, or unique buck numbers on a large parcel based on X # of game cameras per X # of acres.

Ok, while some of you may like the prospects of discussing "advanced math" in the world of whitetails, I would like, hopefully, to take a little less intimidating approach while revealing to you a concept I refer to as "Depth of Cover." Take some time to identify, on paper, the major hunting season food source on your

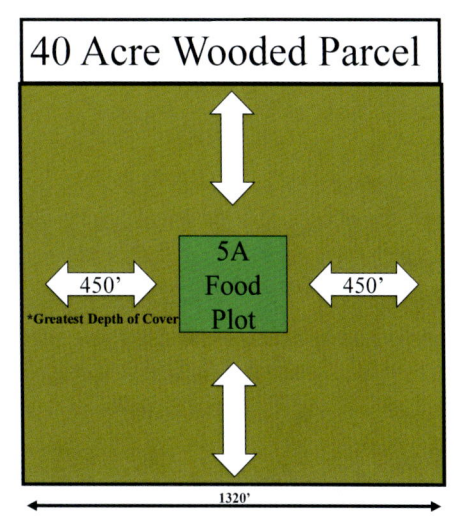

40 Acre Wooded Parcel

450' *Greatest Depth of Cover*

5A Food Plot

450'

1320'
Greatest Length of Parcel

450'/1320' = 34% level of Depth of Cover efficiency

parcel or on your neighbor's. Now, where your cover starts alongside that food source, and where it extends to, whether it is to your property line, your cabin, a lake, or another food source, is your parcel's length of Cover. For example, if you have a square 5-acre food source located in the middle of a 40-acre patch of cover, your length of cover is roughly 450' because you really can't go any further in any direction without running into your property border.

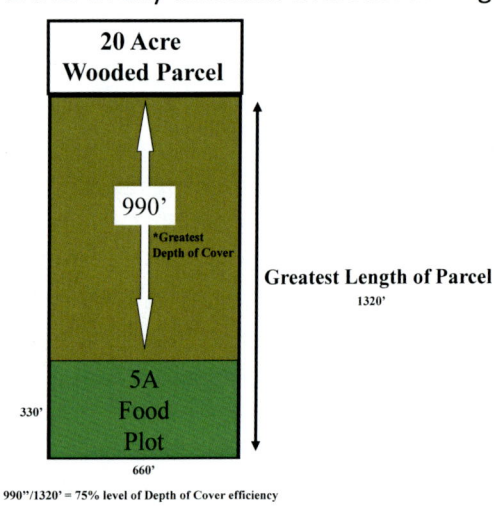

To see how efficient your parcel is relative to its depth of cover, do this: Use the length of cover (450') divided by the total length of a square 40 acre parcel (1320'), and you will find that this example yields a figure of .34, or 34%. A parcel with a 34% level of Depth of Cover efficiency, is very low. On the other hand, a 20 acre parcel with a total length of 1320' featuring a 5 acre rectangular food plot (330'x660') located on one end, features a 75% level of efficiency with a length of cover of 990'. So, using the previous 2 examples, the 20-acre parcel actually offers more than twice the Depth of Cover efficiency level, with more than twice the length of actual cover.

20 Acre Wooded Parcel
990'
*Greatest Depth of Cover
Greatest Length of Parcel
1320'
5A Food Plot
330'
660'
990"/1320' = 75% level of Depth of Cover efficiency

Depth of Cover is something that I have recognized in real world hunting or habitat management situations, both on public and private land, in any state I have worked or hunted in. I am sure there are other ways to explore the efficiency of cover on various types of habitat, but this is a concept that I have been able to apply successfully to a wide variety of whitetail parcels, even when looking back into the lands I hunted over 20 years ago. I am excited to explain to you how using "Depth of Cover" to your advantage can substantially improve your Whitetail Success, so follow along as

I discuss the 4 most important features of this concept, including: Increased daytime bedding opportunity for mature bucks, lower overall deer stress levels, maximum length of quality deer features, and easier hunting!

Increased Daytime Bedding Opportunity by Mature Bucks:

As discussed in later chapters, it appears that doe family groups will frequently bed as close to a consistent food source as possible, and sometimes even within the food source itself, if islands of cover are present. I would ask that you think back to the lands you hunt, and if you have available bedding habitat directly adjacent to a food source, is that habitat typically used by doe family groups, or by mature bucks? At the same time, I have rarely experienced a mature buck bedding between various doe family groups. Is this a scientifically proven practice by mature bucks? I don't think so, but again as in the case of doe family groups if you actually know where a mature buck has frequented a particular daytime bedding area, was it adjacent to a food source, or not?

In the first example of a 40 acre parcel with a 5 acre food plot in the center, the parcel features only a 34% Depth of Cover efficiency level, and at best, only 150 yards to sandwich doe bedding, mature buck bedding, hunter access, and stand locations within. It doesn't take a lot of math to add this scenario up to leaving very little room for daytime mature buck bedding opportunity. Throw in some poor bedding habitat adjacent to the food source, such as an open stand of mature hardwood, and it's possible that first layer of adequate bedding cover isn't available until the parcel border, leaving no room for doe family group bedding, let alone mature buck bedding.

Then there is the 2nd, 20-acre example in which there is 990' of cover to work with outside of the food source. At 660' wide, this is a very large patch of cover to house multiple doe family groups, an adequate amount of cover to house daytime bedding mature bucks, and there is still enough cover left over to use for both exterior hunter access and stand locations. As the season progresses within this orderly establishment of major food source, doe family group bedding, and then mature buck bedding, it's not uncommon that as long as you maintain a low level of hunter/human impact, you will begin to collect pressured deer into their respective bedding area by sex during the hunting season.

Maximum Length of Habitat Features:

The improvements of habitat features that you hunt should rarely be "random" -- meaning, a quality feature of food or bedding here, another over there, with no real connection or relationship of the two. The longer you can link your connections together, the easier it is for you to collect and hold deer, while establishing that natural order of movements. Using the previous 20-acre example featuring a 75% Depth of Cover Efficiency Ratio, a hunter has the opportunity to take advantage of almost 1000' of potential deer improvements. That is literally an awesome length of deer movement, and it doesn't matter if it's only 200 yards wide, 150 yards wide, or even 50, as long as the improvements are secure, consistent, and the deer are hidden within those movements. In contrast, parcels that offer only broken and limited lengths of cover are far less attractive to deer. In fact, when a pressured buck gets to the end of a short length of cover, where does he go? He skips over to the adjacent closest available patch of cover, and he will stay if that neighboring length of cover is large enough to house enough features to provide him the low stress level within a natural order of movement that he craves. If he doesn't find it there, he will move again and again until he is finally killed, or until he reaches that "honey hole" that has the potential to promote him to the age of maturity.

The greatest compliments your neighbors can give you are the bucks that they house and grow all summer, only to have them take residence in your long length of stress-free and unbroken features of deer habitat that you have created. Sound hard? It's not! And what I have found is that the length of that movement, and being able to hide deer within those improvements that make up that movement, is more important than the actual quality of those features within. Too often hunters seek the overall quality level or number of the improvements in the form of food plots, travel corridors, waterholes or deer beds, when reaching a maximum length of unbroken deer features is lacking. When the longest length of cover over a ½ mile (2640') stretch of potential is only 600', there is a lot of wasted space when it comes to attaining whitetail success, not to mention a very poor Depth of Cover efficiency level; but when the table is turned to more closely attain that same parcel's maximum potential length of deer features, "easy hunting" can be found.

Lower Overall Deer Stress Levels:

When your food source is designed to stay consistent in attraction, your bedding cover stays consistent in quality, and the travel corridors feature no gaps in security, the local deer herd experiences a phenomenon that very few deer herds have the luxury to experience. When you can recognize or create this phenomenon, it is a very rewarding experience because you can now enjoy the benefits of a low stress deer movement. It has been my experience that the 2nd, 20-acre example has a much higher opportunity to deliver a low stress deer herd; and without seeing anything else, I would choose to hunt the 20-acre parcel over the 40 if given the chance. A larger parcel alone does not compensate for a poor parcel design unless the acreage is so substantially larger that it is enough to encompass the design flaws.

High Depth of Cover efficiency ratios can lead to lower stress levels...and mature bucks absolutely crave low stress levels. Attempting to establish a natural order of deer movement within short distances is extremely hard, but it doesn't take a giant parcel to accomplish this, just a parcel with favorable length of movement. And this is why some public land parcels can offer some great hunting opportunities where long lines of un-pressured deer movements can be taken advantage of without you as the hunter doing any of the work. I have a particular natural order of movement I can't wait to hunt on a SE OH tract of expansive public land this fall, and basically, I just have to pick the right time of the year, slip in, and pick a few trees. Well, "slip in", after over an hour walk, but you get the idea. When I walk over an hour into that great OH tract of public land, I truly get to an area that I feel "offers it all", including: large food sources, multiple bedding areas, highly defined and secure travel corridors, an extremely long depth of cover, and best of all…a very low level of stress! When you find or create those areas with large food sources, multiple bedding areas, and highly defined travel corridors, I like to refer to them as approaching their "Maximum Length of Deer Features".

Easy Hunting

Is there such a thing as "Easy Hunting"? Have you ever found it? Now please don't get me wrong, it's not all about the kill, spending the least amount of hours in the woods, and watching football the rest of the season, but instead, I like to attempt to be the ultimate predator. What being the ultimate predator means to me is, using knowledge and experience to take a defined and highly efficient approach at harvesting a specific animal or animals that you are pursuing. When you are the ultimate predator in the woods, you are hunting with a sense of purpose that takes the majority of the guesswork out of the equation, while allowing you to kill, "at will".

By using a strong dose of Depth of Cover within the hunting equation, you can find "easy hunting" within a few key areas:

1. Travel. When you know where the local deer herd eats, sleeps, and travels, you as the hunter knows how to move throughout the landscape as a predator would… undetected!

2. Ambush. By defining a natural order of movement through a high depth of cover efficiency, your hunting efforts become highly defined. Where to ambush a mature buck while he beds, while he travels to food, and while he is cruising to and even downwind of known doe family group hangouts, becomes a more efficiently predictable effort.

3. Repeated Opportunity: High depth of cover efficiency parcels leave very little room for "random" and surprised deer usage. The stronger the movement, the better, because deer should, by % of chance, be on the upwind side of you the majority of the time...over and over again. By allowing those movements and usage to be repeated consistently throughout the hunting season over a high depth of cover efficiency, deer become lulled into a false sense of security, while allowing you to observe them over and over again.

Conclusion

Length of Cover and Depth of Cover Efficiency Percentages don't sound like too difficult of calculations, do they? I know that some parcels can become very complex with the variety of irregularity in parcel borders, shapes, and sizes. However, the concept of Depth of Cover is still the same in that by using your greatest length of cover to increase the length of secure deer movements, you can experience many benefits. If your major food source is along the side of your cover...consider moving it to the end to maximize your parcel's overall Depth of Cover Efficiency. There are many ways to improve your Depth of Cover by adding cover or food where needed most.

And, I have to give my High School math teacher, Mr. Brown, some credit! I am still using math today, even a little Geometry and Algebra...much to my displeasure. But, his teaching methods worked, and I have found that by applying just a little "easy math" to the whitetail habitats that I hunt, I can experience a more predictable level of Whitetail Success.

11/30/10 07:40AM MYC

Chapter 8

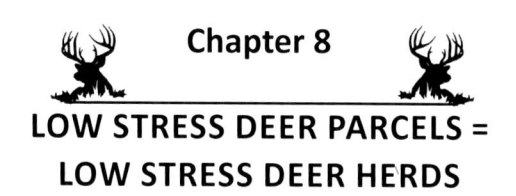

LOW STRESS DEER PARCELS = LOW STRESS DEER HERDS

Pinball machines were just starting to be taken over by video games when I was a kid. It's also too bad, because pinball machines are pretty cool! There are still a few here and there...even one or two are left in the Munising, MI bowling alley my kids play leagues in. What I liked about those pinball games was the hand/eye coordination it took to be pretty good. That little ball would fly around the inside of that machine, bouncing off levers, rails, and bumpers; and the faster the points were racking up, the faster that ball was moving. I can still hear the "ding-ding-ding-ding" repeated in a machine gun cadence that was ever approaching the magical "high score".

That pinball cadence was in my head in 1988 while hunting in MI's "Thumb Area" on opening day of shotgun season. It was the hallowed November 15th and guns were blazing! Over 55 deer per square mile dominated the landscape, and it seemed we had a few miles worth just in our section of land. 10-acre woodlots were more common than 20, and 10 orange coats on a 40-acre parcel were way more common than 2. In the first hour I literally counted over 400 combined shots! I say "combined" because that counted 3-5 round bursts that added up as fast as the "dings" in a good game of pinball. But that's not all that reminded me of the childhood game in which my friends and I would search weeds, bushes, and ditches for hours, finding 10 cent returnable cans and bottles so we could share 1 game.

It didn't take long in those late 80s opening days to fill a doe tag. If you wanted to take a doe and didn't have one down by noon, well...you had missed, and probably a few times. So, by the time 8:00 rolled around I was out of the small thicket of 3 acres of cover I was sitting in, with a doe on the ground, and looking for my brother to aid in a little grunt work. What I saw when I entered the open ground of the expansive harvested ag fields still sits vividly in my head, now 24 years later. A herd of about 15 deer were running across the fields towards my brother at the end of the adjacent woodlot about ¼ mile to the southwest. The excitement was high and it was awesome to be able to watch my brother get a chance... only to miss! I am sure to a 16 year old during his first gun season it was a little overwhelming to see that many deer at 1 time, running right at him! That herd of does and fawns turned and ran along the woods towards the north until "BANGBANG" and the two neighbors shot a couple. The herd turned again and ran ¼ mile to the east to the next woodlot where orange dots filled the woodline and "BANG-BANG-BANG-BANG" the shots continued to ring out, and the ever shrinking herd ran to the next woodlot to the southeast, and then the next over ¾ of a mile away to the south as the few that were left drifted into the safety of a large patch of cover along the sprawling Cass River. I don't know why it jumped out at me so clearly, but it was like one giant pinball game, complete with the cadence of a machine gun and deer being "pinballed" from one bumper of cover, to another.

Can you imagine the stress of that small deer herd? In another chapter of this book I talk about starting deer drives that pushed deer over a mile away by simply walking ¼ mile and then turning around...not even getting within ¼ mile of where the deer were actually being pushed from! By far, those late 80s MI gun season openers were some of the most stressful days of hunting for both hunter and hunted that I can remember. I say stressful for hunters because you haven't seen stress while hunting deer until you hear overhead, tumbling slugs rip through the corn while you take shelter by lying down in the mud between plowed rows of rich, dark soil. So where did those deer end up? Simply, they holed up in the habitat that featured the lowest level of stress, no matter how many acres made up that habitat, and often, no matter how high of quality that habitat was. No Hunters = Low Stress Levels = Piles of Deer, and I am not exaggerating! During late December deer drives, it was not uncommon to have 50 deer run by standers, and my brother was even hit in the leg by one as it went whizzing through the tangle of vines he was hiding in. I can remember one herd that cleared the river bottom after holding in about 15 acres of cover, that had to approach 150 deer. The sound of running deer was amazing! In 11 seasons of hunting the thumb area of MI, I personally passed on 27 small bucks during 1 season alone. Yet in those same 11 seasons, we were only able to see a total of 3 antlered bucks – hunting almost every weekend after the November 15th gun season opener.

BANG BANG BANG BANG….STRESS STRESS STRESS STRESS!!!

Those late 80's weekend hunting trips taught me some extremely valuable lessons about why deer moved, how far they moved, where they moved to and stayed, and why. Whether on public or private land, my new, "modern day" November hunting seasons typically have 1 thing in common; no matter the type of habitat or the state I am in, find the pockets of cover that feature the lowest levels of stress, and find the mature bucks. When deer movements resemble one giant chaotic pinball machine, it is a very bad thing. Buck age structure, sex ratios, hunting effectiveness, and even the ability to harvest does when necessary to keep the populations in check, all suffer. I have found that I have 6 favorite ways to create and protect those pockets of low stress cover. There are other ways to lower stress levels, but these are the most common I employ, and the point I am attempting to make is for you to begin to realize how lowering the overall stress level within the lands you hunt will equal a much higher level of Whitetail Success!

1. Slow the game down. Open woodlots and ag-fields make for a quick pass through movements and high stress environments. Observed body language displayed by deer, show that they stay on edge, they have no reason to stop, and these areas are completely avoided by the local deer herd if possible. I have seen unhunted, open, rolling

hardwoods of 100 acres or more that have become mature buck magnets when the pressure is on, because those parcels still featured low stress hiding spots due to the topography and "lay of the land." Something to consider is the thought that, what you can do on 100 acres of open timber can typically be accomplished on 10 acres or less of improved habitat creations. Expanded fencerows, small habitat islands of ¼ acre or less, pocket or strip cuttings within open hardwoods, or changes in habitat type and age of habitat all serve to slow deer down and eventually hold them. If you can drive an ATV through the woods without having to use a chainsaw, it's not nearly thick enough; and it doesn't mean that the entire woodlot has to be cut down. Instead there needs to be enough layers of a change in habitat that if the 1st or 2nd layer isn't enough...the 9th or 10th one eventually is.

2. Separation of cover. By separating the deer from each other, you can potentially hold more deer. Continuous blocks of unbroken, heavy bedding cover sounds good on paper, but I like to see a clear separation of cover so that the local deer herd can relate to

Mature hardwoods = high stress deer habitat.

that separation as well. An acre of great bedding habitat can often house an entire doe family group of 5-7 deer. If you separate that same acre of bedding into 2, ½ acre bedding areas with an acre of open timber or ag-land in-between, you can potentially hold 1 doe family group in each ½ acre area. Divide that acre of bedding into 4, ¼ acre areas separated by open, deerless habitat in-between...and well, you get the picture. At the same time by offering scattered daytime bedding pockets, a mature buck has to work a lot harder to scent or move about the entire area in search of does. Deer reflect stress from contact with each other as well, so keeping deer apart on your property can possibly reduce the overall stress level. Find those types of areas on public land, and you might have stumbled on to a low-stress honey hole of daytime holding cover.

3. Offer "Sanctuary." Ok, I know the term "Sanctuary" is thrown around very loosely, but let me explain what I believe a true sanctuary is: I have found that a true sanctuary is an area in the whitetail woods where deer cannot see, hear, or smell any hunters moving about the property. The neighbor's dog barking, kids playing in the yard, or even an adjacent bike or walking trail, blend into the normal routines of the landscape because they never contribute to an intrusion into a true sanctuary area. However once that line is crossed…the line between a normal routine and an actual hunting intrusion, the stress level is significantly increased. Noisy equipment or clothing, deer stands, ATVs, and all the smells of hunting that don't fit the normal routine within the areas you hunt, all work to raise stress levels, move deer to seek lower stress levels, and destroy your ability to attract, hold, and hunt deer- in particular, mature bucks, throughout the hunting season. Sanctuaries area a must within any quality hunting area, but I have found that just as easy as it is to create a sanctuary, that same sanctuary can be destroyed within 1 careless moment of intrusion onto your small parcel. By keeping your sanctuary free from all forms of hunter site, sound, or scent…you can allow the lower stress level that you encourage to actually increase your hunting land's deer holding ability as the season progresses.

4. Continuity of Improvements. Your goal should be to hunt areas that feature continuous improvements. During

my travels I have walked some incredible parcels that feature some great holding habitat of solid sanctuary and food on 1 end of the parcel, along with another similar area on the other. Often, these areas have been separated by open, mature hardwoods or ag land, and as I discussed before, a little separation is good when it comes to dividing small pockets of daytime holding deer from one another; but like in most things, too much of a good thing…is bad. When that separation is so drastic that deer rarely cross that opening due to the lack of sanctuary or secure travel corridor, then your hunting grounds become divided. Divide your hunting grounds, especially small hunting grounds of 100 acres of cover or less, and what cover you do have becomes a dead end of movement from your neighbors. You can experience a situation where the typical travel patterns promote a movement back and forth from your neighbor's land to yours instead of being encompassed on yours alone. The smaller your parcel gets, the harder it is to keep this from happening. However, don't let a 20-acre piece of ag land or open hardwoods get in your way! By using strips of grasses, shrubs, trees, cuttings and food to connect your islands of cover, it doesn't take much to offer secure travel across the entire landscape of your parcel. Often converting only 10% of that open ground to secure travel, food, and bedding cover is all that you need to have an effective design. Imagine the difference within the stress of the local deer herd when you can connect even small patches of cover on one end of your parcel to the other, giving the deer the freedom to move about your entire parcel without your site, sound, or scent filtering into their movement patterns. Continuity of Improvements lowers the overall stress levels because deer always have a safe location to turn to within their daily lives on your land.

5. **Orderly Movements by Sex.** If you keep in mind the possibilities of using a food source to locate doe family group and mature buck bedding, you can identify and promote an orderly movement for all deer. When an orderly movement is established, I believe the overall level of stress for the local deer herd is reduced. By first identifying or creating large, consistent fall food sources you can then establish bedding cover for the deer herd. Layers of separated bedding cover is more important than single, large patches of cover because you can successfully attempt to dictate bedding cover by sex. Forget about wind direction as it relates to where a mature buck will bed, but instead try to promote an orderly movement pattern. An orderly movement pattern is beauty to behold! When doe family groups are hitting a major food source early in the afternoon, you can bet those mature bucks won't be too far behind...and if you can maintain that movement with the approach it takes to promote a true sanctuary, you can successfully collect deer into that movement as the season progresses. Even better...the entire deer herd becomes easier to hunt. By establishing an orderly pattern of movement by sex...you are also establishing an orderly bedding pattern by sex. Simply, when you enter the woods you should have a pretty good idea which mature bucks are bedded within which bedding areas, along with the various doe family groups, and you should then have some fairly definitive stand locations to take advantage of that pattern. Through the order of deer movements and bedding by sex, you are establishing a low-stress sense of false security to the local deer herd that allows you to strike with a level of success and efficiency that rivals that of any of the world's ultimate predators.

6. **Reduce the Overall # of Deer/Hunter Encounters.** Every time a deer sees you, hears you, or smells you, is an encounter. When you reduce the number of encounters where you hunt, you potentially reduce the overall stress

level. When you make efforts to substantially reduce the stress level on your parcel, I have found, through experience, that it is most likely that every other parcel in the neighborhood will feature a higher level of stress. It seems relatively easy to do, when in fact it takes dedication at every level, from habitat improvement locations, your access, stand locations, the quietness of your equipment or clothing, and even what kind of scent trail you leave in the woods several hours after you have left for lunch or a late dinner. It's about a general focus of you and your hunting partners, to the point that I like to hear the discussion at the end of a hunt shift from how many deer did you see, to how many deer did you spook. I always pay strict attention to where my hunting partners spook deer, and I stay well away from those areas in subsequent hunts. I have often found that it isn't the "best" stand that yields a mature buck…but the "fresh" stand; in particular, those stand areas that have experienced the least number of deer/human encounters as the season passes by. In fact, a great stand can be destroyed in 1 sit, while a poor stand can be turned into a great stand over time simply by creating an illusion of low stress surrounding that stand location.

7. And of course, "Depth of Cover" is an incredible way to reduce overall stress levels! By using the longest, continuous flow of cover on your parcel to relate to a major food source, you can allow the local deer herd to experience the highest level of space to establish their own behavioral patterns of bedding, feeding, and travel.

Conclusion

My #1 tactic while hunting mature bucks during any state's gun season opener, is to find pockets of cover that feature the lowest level of stress, coupled with some desirable food, bedding and movement features…and hunt. I have found success is there for the taking even on land you have never stepped foot on, just by paying attention to that tactic. On lands that you own or lease, that tactic can be even better because you can actually build and design it yourself. On private land you can accomplish a low level of stress in a very small package that typically requires only a fraction of the acreage that you need to identify on public land because of the high level of quality within those private land improvements that you create.

Pinball games have no place in the deer woods! In fact, due to rampant trespassing and extremely high hunter numbers I happily left my hunting lands of the late 80s to late 90s to explore the wilderness settings of MI's Upper Peninsula. I found a lot fewer deer...but most importantly, a lot fewer hunters, and that was great for my own stress level. I also quickly learned that by taking hunters out of the equation...it became extremely easy to build a high quality, low stress deer herd even in areas with poor habitat, soils, and weather conditions. By reducing the stress levels within the lands that you hunt, deer will come! By providing safe daytime bedding habitat adjacent to consistent hunting food sources, those deer will stay. And when you combine attraction and holding ability on your parcel, you will find that you will experience a very high success rate while creating opportunities to shoot your next buck of a lifetime.

Wisconsin Archery Bucks

Critical Concepts of High Quality Habitat And Hunting Designs

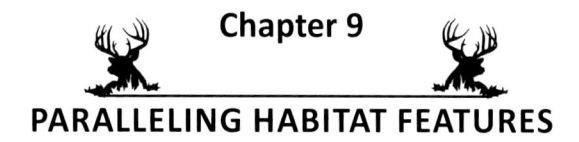

Chapter 9

PARALLELING HABITAT FEATURES

Traveling west on the straight dirt road through the 40-acre parcel I could begin to make out the clearing in the back portion of the property fairly quickly. The landowner and I walked together silently during the mid-summer blue-sky day while the evening temperatures hinted of the upcoming change in season. Deer snorted in alarm just ahead of us and within a few minutes we had made it to the 2-acre food plot located on the extreme western portion of the property. Our approach was exactly that of the typical hunting season approach, and the results were most likely the same...we had just completed a highly effective deer drive of the entire parcel, not to mention, most likely, the neighboring 40 acre parcels as well.

This landowner is not alone. Each year thousands and thousands of landowners make similar mistakes - GREAT looking food plot... poor location - and the same went for the several cuttings the landowner had made on the north and south side of the centrally located access trail. There were some cool looking improvements on the parcel, but of no use, because they were destroyed every time someone entered the parcel. The obvious can be said. The landowner could stay to the outside of the parcel for his access, using the right wind, etc. but that still doesn't solve the problem of the deer being pushed off the property to the west.

As parcel sizes decrease, the distance deer can travel within the improvements of the parcel and how those movements relate to the property borders, become critical. To understand the concept I'm going to discuss in this article, I want you to picture a 40-acre square parcel. That 40-acre parcel will have 4 sides of 1320'. We can begin, on paper, by whittling the parcel down to 1000'x1000' square, exactly in the middle of the parcel, so that there is an approximate buffer of 150' around the border for hunter access. If you, as a land manager, center your improvement efforts of travel, food or cover (Lines of Movement) on the exterior 1000'x1000' border, you now have a potential of 4000' of improvements, or virtually 3/4 of a mile! That's a HUGE difference from the initial example of deer traveling within a chaotic 100 yards of light cover improvements, food, and open woods.

Although that example may be a bit extreme, or sometimes not even possible due to existing natural or manmade features that may not be able to be changed, you have now been introduced to the concept of "Paralleling Habitat Features." What you fit within those improvements, how you access those areas for hunting, and how you maintain the security of those improvements is critical to you as a whitetail hunter.

Parallel Habitat Improvements

Long lines of food, travel corridors, and even the exterior of bedding areas can all be pieces of your parallel habitat features. However, the #1 aspect of all these features has to be, consistency. What I mean by that is that if you have a food source, for example, you can't have holes in nutrition. It does no good to have brassica plantings for the first 400' of the planting, wheat for the next 400', and clover for last 400', if the deer are hammering the clover at the time, and holding off on the rest. The same applies when they are focusing their foraging efforts on the brassica, or even the wheat. Instead, I have found that what has worked best for my clients and me is to have a consistent focus of forage at all lengths of your long lines of food source so the deer continue to move within your parcel confines and have less of a reason to leave. The same is true in most any situation where you are attempting to move deer from point "A" to point "B." These food sources could be as narrow as 10-12' with adequate sunlight, but it is important that you offer multiple forages within the entire length, whether that is a particular forage on ½, and a different forage on the other ½, or even combined together. Try offering something for early in the year and something for late; but most importantly, stretch that variety along the entire length. My current favorite choice for ½ of my plantings in the Midwest is a brassica combo planting, including radishes, rapes, and turnips, with the addition of 25 lbs of buckwheat or soybeans per acre, determined by the overall quality of your soil. On the other ½ of the plot is another favorite of mine - a mix of rye grain, oats, and Austrian Winter Peas. Your blends may vary greatly where you live, but the point is that a combination of plantings used to offer a consistent amount of diversity across the entire length of the line of movement you are trying to create, will continue to keep the deer moving from point "A" to point "B."

The same principle applies to travel corridors and bedding areas as well! There should be no gaps of quality cover that could possibly contribute to deer traveling out of the route that best works for your stand locations, and your hunting access.

There are a multitude of various travel corridor types that will be discussed in chapter 11, but for a typical improvement, consider a 30' wide tangled mess of clearcut running for several hundred feet or more. It's important to weave a deer travel trail through the cutting, maybe even 2-3 trails at times, so that deer can sneak through the improvement. And where will a cruising mature buck be when he is on the downwind side of the inner improvements on your parcel, easily scent checking the interior improvements? He will be right at your feet, choosing not to enter the 50 yard buffer of very few improvements on the exterior of your parcel. That exterior buffer will act as a deer-free approach for your hunting efforts, as well as a downwind blocker to capture your scent within an area that shouldn't typically see a lot of deer activity.

The outside of a bedding area could relate to your parallel habitat feature as well. I strongly advocate screening the outside of your sanctuaries, as well as your targeted bedding areas within those sanctuary areas. So, that outside edge often plays a dual role of both exterior screening to protect the interior bedding activities of the local deer herd, as well as an exterior travel edge for cruising bucks.

When you connect all the pieces together it's easy to see how you can put together 4000' of parallel habitat features. Add a few exterior elbows for ambushing features and various turns and movements around features of topography or natural habitat, and pretty soon you have thousands of habitat features to move your deer WITHIN the confines of your property boundaries.

Easy Access!

By having exterior access trails that use the outside of your parcel, it becomes very easy to take a perpendicular route to access stand locations along your paralleling habitat features. You can position yourself between the outside of bedding area improvements, along a long planted trail plot, or even right up against an improved travel corridor of downed timber, regeneration, and deer trails. Also, because of the long line of improvements, the stand locations can be numerous. You can use each side of your property to approach – following the perfect conditions of wind and seasonal timing.

By seasonal timing, I mean that if you locate some improved bedding areas towards the outside of your improvements, you may want to leave those spots alone to access during the late October, early November period of pre-rut when a mature buck becomes very vulnerable to early morning encounters on the downwind side of bedding areas. Early season hunts may center on food sources, and at the peak of rutting activity, those thick travel corridors can become very productive whether they are located between, food, bedding, or both.

When you access perpendicular to your paralleling habitat features, you take a very non-invasive approach. It is rare that a deer is directly in front of your stand to be spooked by your approach or departure, because you can avoid locations of large food sources or known bedding areas where deer are typically stationary. Also, because you are accessing through typically "non-improved" dead areas, your concerns of scent, site, and sound, as it relates to your intrusion into the habitat, is kept to the bare minimum.

How to Preserve

As mentioned earlier in the book, the fewer # of deer/human encounters on any property you may hunt, the better. A very effective way to accomplish this is through layers of screening cover, basically cover that prohibits the deer on the opposite side from being seen by you, and them seeing you. Thin lines of brush, small ridges, low to medium hinge-cuttings that don't allow the deer to travel through, and even various grasses, including Egyptian Wheat, can be an extremely effective screening of both deer and human movements within your paralleling habitat features.

Also, after you have improved several thousand feet of the exterior of your 40-acre parcel, what about the interior? Interior food sources can be used to funnel deer to the exterior of your parcel or to simply "hide" deer within the confines of your parcel, but many times, intensely improving specifically targeted bedding areas within the interior is a great option for you to take. The entire interior can be improved through the select-cut activities of hardwood species, through overall timber management practices that also improve the quality of the cover and habitat, or through various plantings of cover producing habitat including native grass plantings, conifers, or shrubs; but by targeting small pockets of deer beds and bedding cover, you can offer many options for the local deer herd to bed within your parcel borders. Best of all, you define those interior bedding pockets, and you know exactly where the deer on your property will be bedding! By defining where deer bed within the exact areas you have improved, it makes it a lot easier for you to access along the exterior of your parcel without taking a chance of running into random doe family groups or bucks bedding towards the exterior. It's not that you shouldn't improve the exterior buffer you access through to help preserve your interior improvements, but the closer you are in accessing your parcel borders, the lower the quality of those improvements need to be. That separation of quality will tilt the odds in your favor of truly offering a "deer-free" zone to access through while traveling to stand locations, and to allow your scent to blow into while you are in your stand locations.

Conclusion

Most often you can throw the "perfect" plan right out of the window as topography, exterior influences of food and cover, and even trespassing concerns dictate changes to where your parallel habitat improvements are located. Cookie cutter plans rarely work, so avoid the pitfalls of attempting to fit a potential square peg into a round hole. Now I hope you can at least walk away with the understanding of the concept of Paralleling Habitat Features. As property sizes increase, the paralleling features can be greatly increased as well and used to your advantage to further keep the deer moving about your own property. Deer drives are a tool of the past…and if you effectively learn to implement various parallel habitat features, you may never have to unknowingly participate in a deer drive again!

Chapter 10

LINES OF DEER MOVEMENT

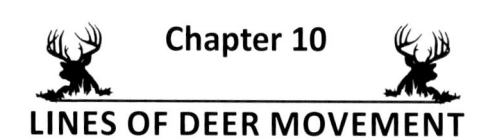

What is a "Line of Movement"? A line of movement is a defined daily travel route between a bedding area to food source, food source to food source, or bedding area to bedding area, between hot spots of deer activity. These lines of movement, and the integrity of those defined lines, are critical to your parcel's holding and hunting ability.

Doe family groups feature some of the most predictable patterns of movement during the hunting season. How many times have you seen a particular doe family group travel the same route, at the same time, to a particular food source day after day during the season? What I have witnessed over a very wide range of deer habitats is that as long as the bedding area and food source stays consistent in attraction...so will the deer movements that relate to that "line of movement." If you can locate multiple lines of movement that relate to each other within the deer habitat that you hunt, then you can expect the doe family groups that use those various lines to be consistent enough to predictably take advantage of them.

Something I have enjoyed throughout the years is getting to know the local doe populations. Although their patterns were much less social during the fawning period, it was always pretty cool to see the various doe family groups pulling back together as fall approached. In 2007, while living in the Central Upper Peninsula of MI, my family and I enjoyed watching "Scar", a 2 year old doe that lost the tops of her ears following a harsh winter, most likely from choosing a bedding area that left her too exposed to bitter temperatures. Scar was 6 years old in 2011, and I learned from the new landowner that she is having her own fawns and is still doing well! Scar's mother is apparently still around, and during the fawning season it was typical to see Scar alone until she joined back up with her mother later in the year. Her mother most often had twins, and my best guess is that she would have been at least 8 years old in 2011. That particular doe family group had a very defined core summer range and core fall range. Typically, outside of the fawning period when you saw one, you saw them all – traveling the same line of movement over and over again.

That consistency of doe family group movements has repeated itself over and over again across the whitetail ranges that I get to know personally. We have a similar group that resides within what we call "The 2-acre field" where I hunt in SW WI. Bedding to water, to small food source, to brushy travel corridor, to major food source, and then back again. That same pattern is repeated by that doe family group to a very definitive level. In fact, if that pattern is not occurring, it doesn't come as a surprise to find out that a mature buck shows up on the camera and has been "pestering" them during the pre-rut or rut, or even that we discover that the neighbor may have been pushing close enough to our property line to spook those deer out of their daytime bedding area while setting up a hunting blind. Because of the consistency of the use of various lines of movement that you can become familiar with, the question shouldn't be, "I wonder if I can shoot a mature doe tonight", but instead, "I wonder which mature doe I should shoot tonight".

Using lines of movement to help unravel the puzzle of whitetail success has been a practice of mine for many years. I have applied it to all of the incredible whitetail memories of my past, as well as to all of the current endeavors of my personal whitetail pursuits for myself, my friends, and my clients. I couldn't be more "sold" on the idea of using Lines of Movement as an important component of your whitetail success.

I have put together the "Top 10 Strategies" for using Lines of Movement to assist you in achieving your ultimate level of Whitetail

Success. When you read through the following, think about not only how these strategies may help you in the future...but how they have helped you in the past...

Top 10 Line of Movement Strategies:

Distance Matters

The longer the distance between high quality hot spots, the easier it is for you to hunt. The reason for that is that you should access the line perpendicular to the movement, so that you limit the amount of time that your movements are possibly exposed to deer moving within that line. Also, when you are accessing the line of movement, and not the hotspots of deer activity themselves (such as bedding areas or food sources), then it is easier for you to access stand positions without spooking the deer within. The further apart the hotspots are, the more likely that you can preserve the hotspot and continue the line of movement, because when you pressure the hotspot, you risk destroying the line of movement. Also, when the hotspots are further apart, the options for using a stand position based on wind direction increases, because as long as your scent is blowing away from the line of movement, you are typically safe.

Thoughts on Random

Random lines of movement on your property can be a major stumbling block to your success. An example of this would be taking an 80-acre parcel, and making it all "cover" by completing massive timber cuttings and other various bedding area related habitat manipulations. Another example of creating random lines of movement is the approach of attempting to improve every square inch of your parcel for deer or wildlife to the point that it becomes very likely that the improvements fail to work together or complement each other. The end result of random lines is a property that is almost impossible to hunt! It can be great if the parcel is never hunted...but of course most of us are hunters. When random lines of movements are employed, then you are left with a parcel that fairly evenly distributes the deer herd across the entire landscape, making it impossible for you to walk in just about any direction without spooking game. The negativity of random movements is less noticeable on a 1000-acre tract or more, because you more closely encompass the daily lives of the local herd, including any unwelcome hunter intrusions into those daily lives. Small parcel random improvements can set traps for you simply because there is little definition to any expected deer movements.

Anchor The Ends

It is very advantageous for a line to be anchored on either end by large hotspots. Depending on your parcel's location, type of existing habitat, and the habitat surrounding your parcel, it may be more important to anchor your lines with large food sources, bedding areas, or a combination of both. Think of those anchoring hotspots as a "dead end" to deer movement, potentially forcing deer to travel back onto your parcel to reach other high quality improvements. Avoid food sources along your property borders unless the neighboring land is of poor bedding habitat, because it is likely, if your neighbor has great bedding habitat, a borderline food source will invite deer to stay on your neighbor's land during daytime hours. Hidden food sources adjacent to large "people areas" of neighborhoods, schools, churches, etc. are a great choice for a "dead end" because the deer are forced to turn back onto your own parcel. At the same time, by building a high quality bedding area on your parcel border, you can effectively roll out the welcome mat for pressured deer that have been pushed around the neighborhood.

Surrounded or Not

Your lines of movement may or may not be encompassed by your parcel. In large ag settings it can be "easy", because huge lines of movement can be attached to surrounding food sources by anchoring those food sources to appropriately located bedding areas within your own parcel. On the "flip-side," wilderness parcels surrounded by remote heavy cover can be difficult to anchor by bedding cover because it's just more of the same and fails to offer a reason for deer to move within the line you are attempting to establish. In remote wilderness settings I have experienced that you can have great success when you attach exterior bedding areas to food sources that have been located on your parcel to establish defined lines of movement.

Strengthen and Defined

Within your parcel borders, lines of movement that are anchored by larger hot spots can be strengthened and further defined in a few ways:

a. small food sources or hunting plots

b. bedding pockets, which usually attract the female portion of the population due to the high-traffic locations

c. creating brush/hinge cut/debris/timber cutting lines that separate outer "non-improved" areas you access through to stand locations, from the improved areas upwind and behind the screening cover to offer a defined edge of movement.

d. "Lay of the land"-could be an inner topography change, open pond or waterway, or any other natural feature that constricts deer movement to complement the line of movement that you are attempting to create.

Poor Access?

A line of movement is a great way to tackle poor access situations. For example, a west to east access is typically problematic because you are entering the parcel traditionally "with the wind." But, with an inner defined line of movement running east/west, flanked by sufficient screening cover on the south and north outer edge of that movement, you then have an effective north and south access for land use and hunting. The more you strengthen the inner line, the more you can potentially re-locate deer from the outer edges of your parcel where you need to access, and into the interior of your parcel where they are safe from your movements.

Dead End T's

Often a line of movement will "T" or "Dead End" into another perpendicular movement; for example, into a large portion of your bedding cover towards the rear or back of your property. This could take place in any direction but it positions you for hunting the inside corners of the "T" as well as the outside sides of the top of the "T" itself.

"Barbell Dead-Ends"

Some parcels contain great bedding cover on both ends. By defining a narrow line of movement between the two, you then create an easier situation to hunt with various wind directions, as well as outside of the bedding cover on either end, depending on access and the time of day. One of my best all-time stand locations features a line similar to this, where movements are constricted but within secure cover between the bedding areas, as well as highly defined.

Screening For Movement

It is critical that all hot spots of deer activity within the line, including the line itself, are screened in some manner. Both bedding and food sources have to be screened effectively to be secure and free from your intrusions into stand locations. Your goal should be to provide very private and secure lines of daily movement for the local herd, so each hot spot has to be protected. It does no good to have the "perfect" bedding or food source if a deer in either of those locations can stand on the edge and see you 50 yards away as you walk by or access stand locations. The stand location described in "Barbell Dead-Ends" includes a very good change of topography that significantly hides hunter's movements to access the location.

Low Risk Access

By hunting the lines of movement, and not the hot spots themselves, you decrease your potential risk of deer/human encounters. A "line of movement" is just that! The deer are traveling in a line from hot spot to hot spot. Unlike a hot spot where a deer may visit a food source or bedding area for hours at a time, a deer instead spends a very brief amount of time traveling within a defined line of movement. Unlike a hot spot where a deer may visit a food source or bedding area for hours at a time, a deer traveling in a defined line of movement only spending a very brief amount of time while passing through. Of course, a deer will stop to browse, or a buck may be successfully slowed down by providing mock scrapes within the line adjacent to stand locations, but by hunting a line of movement you expose yourself only a fraction of the time, in comparison to hotspot locations.

Conclusion

The key is DEFINING the lines of deer movement so that you take the guess-work out of where the deer travel, and where you can effectively enter and exit the property that you hunt. And when you do access a stand location along a line of movement? It's a great idea to access through mature timber, or even through an exterior portion of habitat that is a much lower level of quality than your interior improvements. If you do access a stand location along a line of movement, it is a great idea to access through mature timber, or even through an exterior portion of habitat that is at a much lower level of quality than your interior improvements. By doing this, you will be able to keep the deer where you need them... as well as where you don't need them.

The ultimate goal is to put all of those lines of movement together within a cohesive unit that gives your property the optimum daily travel pattern encompassing as many appropriately located hot spots as possible. But, it's not as easy looking at the "perfect" property layout on paper. Instead, there are no "perfect" property layouts, and every parcel is different in many ways! Every exterior and interior influence needs to be considered. Neighboring bedding areas, neighboring food sources, neighboring funnels, travel corridors, waterways, houses, roads, age and type of timber, etc., are all features that need to be taken into consideration to effectively establish and hunt the lines of movement that are necessary for the success of your parcel.

These lines of movement are one of the most important aspects of property management I assist my clients with. Often the success of the parcel or hunting location isn't created because of the perfect bedding area or food source...but instead, your level of whitetail success will often directly relate to how well you establish and maintain the integrity of the lines of movement on your parcel. It has been my experience that maintaining the integrity of the existing lines of movement on the lands that you hunt, is often more important than the improvements you make to strengthen those lines. I have seen some great locations that didn't feature any human improvements, including the location for the story used within the intro of this book...

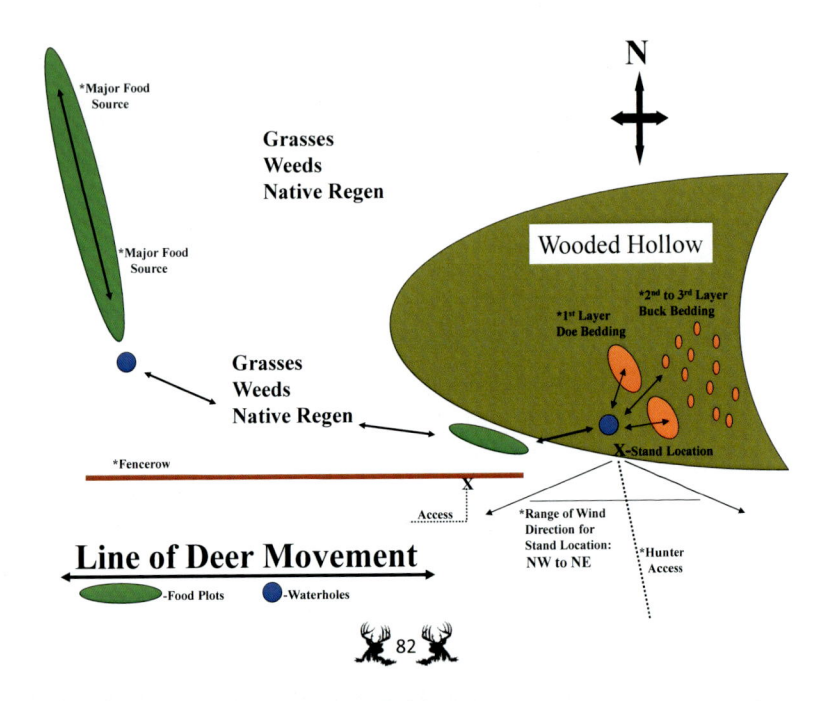

*Major Food Source

Grasses
Weeds
Native Regen

N

Wooded Hollow

*Major Food Source

*1st Layer Doe Bedding

*2nd to 3rd Layer Buck Bedding

Grasses
Weeds
Native Regen

*Fencerow

X-Stand Location

Access

*Range of Wind Direction for Stand Location: NW to NE

*Hunter Access

Line of Deer Movement

-Food Plots   -Waterholes

Chapter 11
HIGH POWERED BUCK TRAVEL CORRIDORS

Back in 1999 I purchased 120 acres of tag alder thickets, spruce and fir swamps, and sandy loam soil filled with 15-year-old white, red, and jack pine regeneration. To say that this parcel was "thick" was an understatement. I have to smile when my southern MI habitat management brothers suggest that, "It can't be too thick!" Trust me, I've seen cover so thick that anything much larger than a rabbit needed a machete and a wood-chipper to take a walk.

Throughout the next few years I soon learned that deer quickly used ANY cover that was removed, to make way for a stand access trail. Pocket-cuttings of conifer bedding islands and deer travel tunnels, became the tools of choice to funnel deer use exactly where I needed it to be. In fact, all of the trails that accessed a treestand had to feature a dead-end at the stand, or deer would begin to use them immediately. During the last few years I found that using "gates" of horizontal pole-timber cuttings left at various heights, made for great deterrents to unwanted deer traffic at the entrance of stand access trails.

Taking those experiences with thick brush and deer usage, it wasn't too difficult to apply that to any area I wanted to strengthen a line of movement between deer hot spots of food or bedding cover. Deer LOVE to move through thick corridors of low brush and high timber stem counts per acre. For example, a young aspen thicket can contain 8000 shoots or more per acre, and when you cut out a 2-3 foot trail from a bedding area on one side, to a food source on the other...guess where the deer travel? Layered Timber Cuttings, Chainsaw Corridors, and Deer Tunnels, are some High Powered Creations that I often recommend to my clients. I'm looking forward to telling you how you can use cuttings, corridors, and tunnels to compliment the next great line of movement on your parcel!

Layered Timber Cuttings

I recently had the opportunity to work with a very good forester whose firm covers the region of IA, IL, and SW WI. I designed a property layout for an IL client, and part of the design included the need to harvest a portion of the mature timber located on the parcel. The forester recommended a plan that included cutting approximately 20 acres of timber under a forest management plan that he was developing. That particular cutting included the bulk of the timber within the heart of the parcel and both the landowner and I were reluctant to encourage a total harvest percentage that high at this time. The landowner was more comfortable with 7-8 acres of cuttings that we could use to be a little more strategic, and the forester agreed to come up with an alternate plan. What we came up with together, is something I like to refer to as "Layered Timber Cuttings." The forester wanted to cut a block of timber...or something close to a block of cuttings, but again, the landowner's goal was to develop his property for deer hunting and deer management, so a large block was not appropriate in his situation. Right now as we speak the loggers are in the woods...and a forestry plan was developed in accordance with the State of Illinois that will now be used to move deer across the landowner's parcel exactly where he wants them to be.

The area to be cut features a large bowl of topography with an outside rim approximately 1500' in length. This outside rim contains a large professionally installed bedding area on the east end centered around a rocky point with a series of small benches, then travels to the west where a new waterhole has been installed for hunting opportunities, and then finally cuts to the southwest, ending at another professionally installed bedding area on a high, rocky point. With a 200' cutting width, the total acreage cut will be around 7 acres, and the outside upper edge of the cutting will be used as a hard edge that separates mature timber above from the layered clear-cut below. The mature timber above will be maintained as "Old Growth Forest" to be used for hunter access and downwind blocking for stand locations for the foreseeable future.

During the cutting operation the loggers are leaving the undesirable timber species on the ground within the outside edge of the cutting to offer immediate horizontal surface structure, and then will be cutting a small 2-3' deer trail through the debris to establish a highly defined deer corridor. The landowner is following up by planting hundreds of conifer species within that outer mess of cut timber to create permanent corridor exactly where he needs it to be. The process takes several steps, but in the end the new 1500' layered cutting will offer an immediate impact in the definition of deer movements while offering a highly defined corridor for many decades to come. Two subsequent cuttings will take place every 8-10 years, with the interior north edge of the most southern cutting, and the southern edge of the northern cutting, making a fairly straight line edge that meets up on the west side installed bedding area to further complement the intended lines of movement. Also, that same interior cut line travels out the east edge of the woods and meets up with the start of a native grass travel corridor that heads south and east to large food plots being established within a distant pasture.

Thin and long is most appropriate in many habitat improvements, and timber cuttings are no exception, especially if you desire the deer to travel exactly where you need them to be for optimal hunting opportunity. There are additional reasons thin and long is a very good practice in the whitetail woods and the next practice really sheds some light on that thought.

Chainsaw Corridors

Let's have some fun! With safety in mind, fire up the chainsaws and design your corridor with a 30-50' cutting through low value timber, and let it lay. I like to cut anything over 6 inches; and what is the best direction to cut? Whatever way the tree will fall safely...

With a cutting like this you are attempting to connect "Point A" with "Point B." Those two points may be food sources, bedding areas, or any combination of the two, including natural or manmade. The outside of the cutting is for hunters...the inside for deer. Like in the above example of the layered timber harvest, the exterior mature timber offers a great "deer-free" buffer for access and downwind blocking while on stand. A typical buffer may be around 100' from a parcel border...always running parallel to your border to encourage deer to stay on your own property - not perpendicular so that deer are pushed off your parcel. Also, the chainsaw corridor is impossible to see through...giving you an incredible separation between yourself and the deer. You can access a stand location virtually right on top of the corridor, and a deer 40 yards in either direction has a very difficult time discovering your approach.

After your cutting has taken place, it's not complete without a couple of enhancements. A 2-3' deer trail notched out through the path of least resistance in the middle of the cutting, gives you an exact trail the deer will follow; and the remaining trees of 6 inches or less can be used to hinge and tie to produce a tunneling effect over your new deer trail. The next step is the addition of conifer species for a permanently defined travel corridor within hardwood species, and by reducing canopy in and around your cuttings, you can be assured of plenty of sunlight.

It's a great idea to locate bedding areas on the inside edge of the corridor and then stand locations at least 40-50 yards away from those areas. You can narrow down exactly where you expect deer to be bedded while going into a stand for an afternoon sit, and you can greatly reduce your chances of spooking deer. Also, mature bucks love to cruise on the downwind edge of bedding areas through an edge of habitat change, which puts them right at your feet within the 2-3' deer trail that your created.

Deer Tunnels

Do you already have young cuttings, low canopy, and high timber stem counts per acre…possibly even heavy conifer cover? Well creating some tunnels might just be for you. Using "Deer Tunnels" through heavy tag alder and conifer cover on my 120-acre parcel had some amazing results. It was incredible how the deer traveled exactly where I wanted them to, entering food plots and using bedding area travel routes in a highly defined manner. Most of the time it was only a matter of trimming a 2-3' deer trail through heavy cover, from the level of my chest and down. The cuttings created a tunnel effect, and a spring created tunnel would routinely feature rubbing activity within the first season.

It's pretty easy for you to expand that practice to low brush, tag alder, and hardwood regeneration settings as well. For example, you can have a great time pulling down and tying small 10-12' saplings towards each other to create a tunnel effect. Each tie then complements the next, and pretty soon a tunnel of 60 yards long and crossing exactly where you want it, within close proximity to a stand location, becomes a highly defined travel corridor. You can also use your imagination! One of my personal favorite things to do is to "capture" deer movements from a bedding area or food source by taking several trails and connecting them down to 2, and then finally 1 that travels by your stand. On an inside field corner edge, it's a great idea to form an "X" just upwind from where your stand location is, with multiple legs of deer tunnels working to move deer at a precise location.

By continually maintaining your tunnels you can carry a lush growth of low vegetation across the entire length. Simply tie down any new growth every couple of years while adding to the tunnel from the outside, and the results can be outstanding. Add some well-placed conifer or shrubs along the entire tunnel and you can offer a more long-term effect.

Conclusion

If your property is so thick that small animals have to use machetes and wood-chippers...you may want to give up and hunt elsewhere. However for the rest of you, consider the positive effect of giving the deer an easy way to move throughout your woodlots. I was simply amazed at how effective cutting corridors began to move deer freely throughout my 120 acre parcel, and I've seen that pattern of deer usage repeat itself across the entire Midwest, whether it's within conifer, hardwoods, low brush, or natural timber regeneration. Don't leave the deer movements up to chance; instead, pick up a chainsaw and a length of nylon cord and have some fun!

Chapter 12

HABITAT STEMS PER ACRE

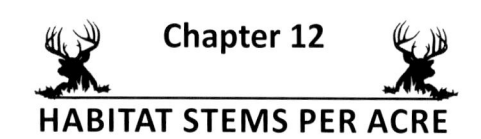

Using changes in habitat is described in Chapter 6 is one way to break down a large chunk of public land for a quick scouting trip. Another easy way to take 10,000 acres of mature public land hardwoods and narrow it down to where the deer are going to be, is to look for the most "stems per acre," meaning, the highest density of saplings, bushes, weeds, etc. Even areas that feature poorer soil that cause the trees to be stunted and smaller in diameter, actually allowing more trees in one location, can be the difference that makes the deer feel more comfortable. Preferred fawning cover has always featured the most stems per acre, while promoting scent dispersion and escape cover.

From newborn fawns to maturity, I have experienced that deer prioritize the density of stems per acre for both where they choose their bedding cover, and how they travel about the land they have chosen to call home. And if you think of some of the best bedding areas you have come across, it doesn't necessarily mean that deer can't see 10' in front of them, as in the case of a conifer thicket; it simply means that they have the level of security within stem density to feel completely hidden - and they are! When you tuck a deer back on a small hump within a tag-alder swamp, they are virtually impossible to see at 20 yards. Not only can a deer be completely hidden in these situations, but they also typically enjoy a much higher amount of food per acre!

A one-acre clear-cut can produce up to a thousand of pounds of forage per acre. WOW...that's an incredible amount of food compared to a mature stand of timber! I spent some time with a fellow deer nut in October of 2010, and as a local in this SW WI ag region, he was really excited about the prospect of the corn seemingly maturing at a higher rate this year; even the leaves already starting to turn into their tanned coats of fall. He was excited because as most Midwest hunters know, when the corn is up, it can be extremely hard to shoot a mature buck because they can spend so much time in the standing corn. Those rutting bucks have ample food, a huge supply of cover and security, and does, all in one location! Can you blame them for staying put? Not to mention, thousands of stems per acre!

Whether it be scouting for your next hunting location, improving your bedding areas, or zeroing in on a red-hot clear-cut featuring a bounty of fresh young growth, by focusing on the stem per acre count, you will be much closer to reaching hunting and management success.

The Thicker, the Better?

With all this focus on stems per acre, it may seem that thicker is always better - right? Well, not exactly. I've been on small islands of cover in northern MI where the spruce and fir were so thick only a snowshoe hare took residence. On the other hand, I have found that I could take those same islands of cover, cut a few small openings within, cut some connecting trails, and finally cut a few escape routes and the next year not only would a few rubs pop up on the inside of the island, but on the outside of the island as well, as deer had started utilizing trails to and from their new bedding area. And that situation is no different with areas of low hinge-cuts or blow downs, in that too much horizontal cover (as in the case of the lower conifer branches) can make it almost impossible for a deer to utilize the space. So when I'm referring to stems per acre, again, I'm referring to the amount of vertical cover, even if horizontal structure is still useful much of the time.

There are a number of situations where a high stem count per acre can occur naturally. For example, in a cedar swamp there is often the edge of change in elevation where a different soil condition and amount of sunlight encourages more variety in habitat, translating into more stems per acre. Of course the south-facing slopes of rolling hardwoods are always a good bet for an increase in stems per acre, as well as the outside edge where uplands meet lowlands; and the change in soil moisture and soil type encourages a transition of diversity. Think of all the great bedding habitat found along the many ditches and waterways that traverse the small woodlots and patches of cover in the large agricultural regions. Flood plain areas that transition into uplands along the bottoms, can often be a tangled mess of vines and water-pushed piles of deadfalls, combined with small humps, bumps, and ridges filled with grasses that offer a unique variety. Finally, I can't leave out the countless patches of sumac that dot the landscape along many of our Midwestern highways. Some people like to play "I spy something…" when driving, but instead, I like to play the "find the rub in the sumac along the highway" game.

Often it's not the center of those hidden patches of high stem counts that will lead you to success, but the outside, where the change in habitat creates an edge that deer like to travel through or against. That edge will give to you a definitive travel pattern, and if you connect that edge to another that forms an intersection, and hunt on the downwind side, you can often find a real hotspot to hang a stand. Often it's just a matter of waiting for the deer you are after to come out of the interior of their bedding areas created by the high stems count, to utilize the line of habitat edge that you are anticipating their travel on.

Bedding Insulation

An extremely good bedding area I was familiar with around 20 years ago, was a small tag alder swale totaling less than 2 acres, surrounded by a field on 3 sides and small wood lot on the other. On the outside of the field area on each side, there was a heavy fencerow. In total, the area included about 5 acres and routinely held over 20 deer. The nearby 20 acre woods would often hold less than 5 deer, and it probably comes as no surprise that the amount of stems per acre in the 2 acres of tag alder bedding area was close to or possibly even more than what the entire 20 acres held. But the beauty was in checking out the inside of the bedding area!

Being "young and dumb" we routinely drove deer out of that small patch of cover, and although we managed many more misses than deer, I was always the one pushing, and I couldn't help but pause to look around the bedding area...it was always such a sacred place to me! What the 2-acre bedding area included was a tag alder canopy about 10-12' high, with a network of trails and small "rooms" of bedding cover. Often the best way to start a drive was to sneak to the outside of the fence row on the north side, take a few steps while breaking some brush, and the entire herd was already out the south side. Once I would walk through the fencerow, any stragglers could see me through the outside of the bedding area and would take off.

The beds themselves were completely open with none of them being any larger than a small pick-up. They were dry and were full of flattened dead grass. A bedded deer on the inside could see outside in some directions, but the heavier fencerow of briars, grass, vines, and old apple trees kept them completely hidden.

Keep that scenario in mind when thinking about quality bedding areas you are either looking for, or trying to construct on your property. Your success will not be found in the bed itself, but by what type of vertical stems per acre cover surrounds the beds. That vertical cover is what is actually supporting the bed in the first place, and without it, the "bed" is just another small lowdown in the woods, rarely used except by the most displaced subordinates within the herd. On a larger scale, think of an entire bedding area, including many man-made or natural deer beds. Often a prescription for a 15-acre bedding area within a stand of mixed age hardwood, might be to harvest the marketable timber, and to use a portion of the pole timber left standing, along with cut tops and debris, to construct deer beds within the fresh growth that will be generated by the cuttings. You then have the insulation of stems per acre to surround your bedding construction efforts; and if you add an outside layer of native grasses to surround the 15 acres, the entire deer herd is completely insulated by stems per acre. At the same time, there will be an incredible explosion from a new food source!

A Clearcut Bounty

I read an article at least 10 years ago that talked about hunting a fresh clear-cut like you would a cornfield. Coming from primarily an agricultural hunting background, that was of particular interest to me. And yes, the same tactics worked, whether it be setting up on the outside travel corridors as deer traveled in and out of the clear-cut to feed, or hunting on the downwind side as buck came cruising through to scent check the area. It is not the case all of the time, but often you will find that as the stem count increases, so does the amount of food.

By strategically locating 20 acres of cuttings within a 40-acre parcel, the local deer herd can experience 20,000 lbs. of new, fresh growth! And when that sunshine hits the forest floor, that in the past only provided 50-100 lbs. of forage per acre, there can be a huge increase in not only the amount of forage, but in the variety as well! All of a sudden a hunter has a lot to work with in terms of a destination of food source, cover, and newfound edge habitat for predictable deer travel routes.

Conclusion

"Stems per Acre" is not a new concept, but maybe you've never thought about how it applies to your hunting efforts? Thinking back to those premium fawning grounds, there has been some speculation in the past that a mature buck just may travel back to those sacred high stem count hideouts when the pressure really heats up! That mature buck is simply going back to what makes him feel safe, and I think that emphasizes the importance of focusing on stems per acre for your hunting and/or management efforts. And for your next quick public land hunt in the open hardwoods...try locating the most stems per acre first and see what kind of deer sign you run into!

Pictorial Tips and Tactics for Whitetail Success

What a difference a year makes! This "morning double" features a couple of bucks that appear pretty closely related. Can you tell which one is the three year old and which one is the four year old? The concepts discussed within this book can help you advance the overall age structure of the bucks on the land you hunt.

Don't let poor soils get in the way of a good food plot location. Instead match your seed selection to the conditions and experience success. The rye grain planted below was just what this location needed to continue the line of deer movement between bedding cover and a major food source.

After "sitting dry" all day deer often gravitate to a water source before continuing to travel to an evening food source. Don't let the lack of a water source on your property get in the way of success. Instead, try using containers to define the travel patterns for the deer on the land in which you hunt.

When populations are not in balance with the local habitat, antlerless harvest is biologically critical, and at the same time can make room for more bucks on the lands you hunt. Don't expect mature bucks to reside in your area if doe family groups dominate the landscape.

Above: Minnesota native grass field
Below: Northern Michigan conservation conifer planting

Below: Avoid plantings of single habitat types for bedding cover. Instead, include a variety of habitat types to improve the diversity and attractiveness of the daytime bedding cover on your property

Above: Southern Michigan natural deer bedding cover.
Below: Central Michigan man-made bedding cover.

It's not to difficult to mimic natural deer habitat conditions. With an open mind and a little elbow grease you can provide what the deer are lacking within your area.

August 13, 2012: 14 Days of growth and this planting is well on it's way to producing an outstanding fall food source that has the potential to meet the cool season needs of the local deer herd, within an extremely short growing season.

August 31st, 2012: Only 18 days later, and 32 days of growth! This food plot combination of grains and brassicas will provide a high-volume cool-season treat to nearby bedded whitetails during a critical period of the year: November.

Ribbons of green in Southwest Wisconsin.

Long lines of planted food sources can be used to hide deer while hunters access tree stand locations, as well as to define exactly where deer travel across your property.

The ability to hide a food plot from the "sight, sound, and scent" caused by hunter access...

...is more important then the quality or type of forage planted within that food plot.

Above: Man-made deer beds offer the ability for the land owner to definitively predict where deer spend their daytime hours.

Above: Don't let wet areas get in your way of a good deer bed. With a pallet, buckets of sand, soil, and a shovel, an adequate bedding platform can be offered within fairly poor habitat conditions.

Hunting over small water holes can often be a more successful option then hunting over a food plot because deer spend a very short time drinking before traveling to another destination. This will limit your possible exposure to traveling deer.

Mature bucks often move during daytime hours. Instead of focusing on if the **local buck population** is nocturnal or not, concentrate your efforts in keeping your **hunting lands** from being nocturnal. Make sure that you attempt to establish a low stress atmosphere for the local deer herd.

2004 planting of rye, brassicas, clover, and chicory.

Right: Spring of 2005 following a 2004 late summer planting of Oats, Clover, and Chicory.

Below: 2012 late summer planting of buckwheat, oats, and soybeans

Combo plantings are critical for maintaining a consistent focus by the local deer herd throughout the entire hunting season. Consider "side by side" combo plantings with 2 different base forages such as brassicas or grains for the ultimate level of diversity and consistency in deer usage.

Got Hills? There are several ways to use hills to your advantage:
1. Hidden access
2. Downwind Scent Control
3. To hide deer within remote bedding points or benches
4. By taking advantage of topography features that constrict deer movements such as steep drop-offs, benches, and saddles.

Experience whitetail success while creating memories to last a lifetime with family and friends.

"The Wide Eight"

Four Year Old

Five Year Old

Six Year Old

Addressing the needs of both food and cover during the most critical periods of the hunting season can give you the opportunity to attract, hold, and hunt a buck of a lifetime.

Chapter 13

SCREENING COVER

I'd like you to picture the "perfect" bedding area within a remote portion of a parcel located in a fairly level agricultural region. OK, it was more than level - it was downright flat, and that only added to the predicament I'm going to share with you. The bedding area was well designed with recent hardwood cuttings and located in an "out of the way" spot towards the rear of the parcel. "On paper" the bedding area appeared to be set for attracting and holding a "cover-starved" local deer herd. However, there was a problem, or you probably wouldn't be reading this story.

You have probably all heard of screening cover before, and its name implies exactly what it does. Screening cover creates a visual barrier to hide the deer from you, and you from the deer. One of my most common, current screening cover recommendations, is to plant Egyptian Wheat, a fairly drought tolerant plant that looks similar to corn when mature, stands up very stiff under the weight of heavy snow, and reaches heights of over 12'. Egyptian Wheat is a great example of a habitat screen! How extensively do you use screening cover within your property's habitat management program? Are your access trails screened from your property's deer herd? What about your stand locations, bedding areas, food sources, your hunting lodge, or possibly where you park and access your property? Come to think of it, just about every hot spot of deer or hunter activity should be screened on your property, and the previously described client's bedding area was no exception. Also, that same thought can often apply to many designated sanctuaries located on deer hunter's properties, and without a good foundation of effective screening cover, your entire property can become a pinball machine of chaotically disturbed deer activity.

What exactly was the problem with that agricultural bedding area screening cover, or lack thereof, you might ask? Well, the #1 problem was that it was too exposed "to the rest of the world." As a hunter attempted to enter the edge of the woodlot into the wind through an adjacent idle open field, a deer on the edge of the bedding area, approximately 75 yards into the woods, could see the approaching hunter from over 400 yards away! Because there was no topographical change, there was also no better way to approach the woodlot, so the hunter could potentially be seen from any direction. Worse yet, the hunter was never even close enough to know just how many deer he had the potential of spooking because the deer were gone long before the hunter arrived.

One way I knew these deer would not be there in this situation was because I had driven deer on similar land I had hunted in the late 80's and early 90's. A 5-acre woodlot was ½ mile from the farmhouse we parked our vehicles at. One mile to the east was another road with a ditch traveling ¼ mile west to the end of a long and skinny 10-acre woodlot, connected by a small ditch to the 5-acre wood lot that faced the farmhouse. The "drive" was a simple one and started by dropping off a hunter with a bow during the late season and giving him enough time to walk the ¼ mile ditch, and then to get into position in front of a small knoll that shielded his position from deer that would be driven from the west. Then, my job was to simply start walking across the ½ mile ag field while approaching the 5-acre woodlot, hoping to drive deer to the waiting bowhunter. "Believe it or Not," the walk rarely lasted even ½ the way to the 5-acre woodlot until a distant yell or radio contact would notify me that the deer had already been driven by the hunter ½ mile away and the hunt was over. It happened that fast with just ¼ mile walk, still ¼ mile from the woodlot; and it didn't take much imagination to understand what was going on with my client's "perfect" bedding area described above.

As you continue reading I am going to give you a brief description of the types and uses of screening cover, and see how that open ag bedding area could be easily fixed to begin attracting and holding a portion of the local deer herd.

Description

There are numerous types of screens that can be used to shield your movements from the local deer herd. Changes in topography, brushy fencerows, conifer plantings, logging debris, hinge cuts, various grasses, weeds, Egyptian Wheat and even standing rows of corn, all have their place in the world of screening cover. Also, "too much of a good thing is not a good thing" can actually be the case when it comes to screening cover. Screening cover is not bedding cover! If your screening cover is starting to attract bedding activity then one of a couple of problems exists. 1. The screening cover is too wide, or 2. The quality of your interior bedding area the screening cover is adjacent to, is not good enough. So, a critical component of screening cover is that it does not become bedding cover and it is as straightforward as its name implies. It is simply "screening cover."

Real World Application

First and foremost a bedding area isn't a bedding area without effective screening cover. On large parcels of 500 acres or more, a hidden bench or point may act as bedding cover even when surrounded by 20 acres or more of open hardwoods, but on small parcels you just do not have the luxury of having 1 bedding area for every 20 acres. So an effective bedding area, or cluster of deer beds, begins with adequate screening cover on the exterior. Then, by offering screening cover you can define numerous bedding areas or even individual beds. An example of effective screening cover within a hardwood setting would be, knee to waist high hinge cuttings on the outside of the bedding area(s), and then chest to shoulder high hinge cuts can be used on the inside to allow for movement and increased canopy cover on the inside of the bedding cover. However, the need for screening cover as it relates to a bedding area does not end there.

An often overlooked aspect of screening cover is when you use it to screen your movements as a hunter when walking by a bedding or feeding area. Screening cover should still be used on the exterior of each management feature, such as a food plot or bedding area, but then the real security comes in when human movements are also shielded from view. Something else that happens in this scenario is the fact that your sound will carry much less when muffled by an effective screening cover, such as rowed conifer plantings or a handy ridge system. One of my preferred methods of access for my northern MI parcel is by the use of a ridge system that rises more than 100' higher than the adjacent hunting areas and food plot systems. The ridge system offers the perfect "screen" to shield both the site and sound of my approach.

Another potentially missed opportunity when it comes to screening cover is at the actual stand location. You may have been able to walk by bedding areas that have been defined by exterior screening cover, your approach could be undetected due to a thin line of rowed conifer plantings, but at this point it all boils down to your stand site. Is your stand access screened as well? I personally rely on this aspect of screening cover so much that with any permanent blind or tent I use, I literally cannot see into my shooting lanes until I get into the blind, and look out a window. It might be a large brush pile that you have to look through as it lays in front of your blind, a small ridge your shooting house is set behind, or possibly you have been fortunate enough to locate a conifer "hidey-hole" of young growth to shield the entrance of your blind location, but the use of screening cover for stand access is critical.

Also, you can be creative! I had one 2007 client that used an excavator to not only build 10-12' berms along his entire road frontage and sanctuary, but to also build a series of mounds in and around his potential bedding areas to even further hide the local deer herd from his movements. In 1995 I actually had a local contractor construct a 6' high berm alongside my truck camper. I then planted a row of spruce trees on top to shield my movements while I dressed and got ready in the otherwise open terrain, before I accessed my stand location.

Do you want to make your small property to appear much larger than it is? By offering screening cover you define layers of habitat change that offers an increase in security for the local deer herd whether they are taking daytime refuge within a hidden bedding area, or getting a bite to eat on a secluded food source. It's actually much harder to think of a situation where screening cover is not appropriate, than when it is, so use your imagination! Does anybody have an outhouse next to your cabin?

Conclusion

So what was the problem with the "perfect" bedding location discussed at the beginning of this article? Well, nothing was wrong with the actual bedding area; it was the lack of screening cover on the outside of the woods that was needed to further insulate the bedding cover from human intrusion. A row of conifer, a line of low to medium high hinge cuts, maybe even a 20' wide path of native grasses planted on the outside of the woodlot, could all turn into an adequate shield to screen hunter movements from the interior bedding activities of the local deer herd. To get a little fancy, a combination of young conifers that will eventually offer a permanent screen starting in 12-15 years, flanked by native grasses, along with a series of hinge cuts just inside the edge of the woodlot, would offer an effective screening plan for not only the next hunting season, but for decades to come. Effective screening cover shouldn't be just an afterthought; it should be the foundation of almost every habitat feature you wish to create or enhance on your small parcel. If a stand location, food source, or bedding area seems to be missing something on your property, consider whether you have done an adequate job in screening your human activities from the local deer herd. In the end, a bedding area without screening cover is not much different than a bathroom without walls - even deer need a little privacy!

11/04/11   11:25AM

Chapter 14

BEDDING LAYERS FOR MATURE BUCKS AND DOES

Bucks, bucks, bucks…P&Y, B&C, 10 points, 12 points, total inches, total mass…beam length, tine length, total spread. Now seriously, how many campfire tales surround the mysterious ways of that really cool doe on the property? "Big Moe," the "Big 8," "Slick," "Tall Boy," "Heavy 10"…is it safe to say we focus at least a little on bucks? Not that there is anything wrong with that…But in reality it doesn't matter if you are hunting on public or private lands. It all starts with the females, and I'm not talking about sex ratios, populations maintained in balance with the habitat, and all of the other indicators of herd health. By starting to think and focus on the doe family groups and where they are positioned on the lands you hunt or manage, your efforts can then all fall into place. I'm going to tell you how, but as I've found in my own life, if you don't put the ladies first…it's just not going to work out very well.

Ask yourself for a second…How many men hang out at the beauty shop, shopping malls, bridal showers, baby showers, candle parties, etc.? Hey, we men have our own things, right? Ball leagues, poker nights, Monday Night football…. Sometimes the ladies are around, and personally, I think that's a pretty cool thing! But, the point is…gals have their times…guys have theirs. So, think of how that relates to the property you hunt. IF the women rule the roost and are left to wander across the entire tract, where do the guys go? Is there even any room left for mature bucks where you hunt?

Let me give you an example of an 80-acre parcel that you approach from the long side…basically a 40 to your left, and a 40 to your right. In the center is a great 10-acre food plot surrounded by some of the most beautifully matured hardwoods one could have.

80 Acre Hunting Parcel

- Scattered Buck Bedding
- 1st Layer Doe Bedding
- 10 Acre Food Plot
- Mature Hardwoods
- Mature Hardwoods
- ---Hunter Access---
- House
- County Road

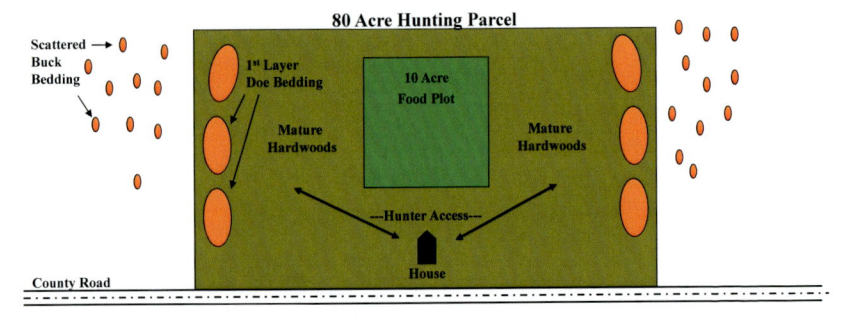

By the time you drive in to access your garage, and then cross the food source...you essentially reach the back of your property line. Cut through the open hardwoods to the left and you have about 15 acres of heavy cover along the parcel border to the west...and then to the right and towards the other border you are left with about 20 acres. The 10-acre field is a HUGE draw and carries with it a high attraction of a sizable deer herd within the area. Those deer come from either end of the property to feed towards the center... returning at daybreak back to the outsides of the parcel to bed until evening. In essence, this parcel is being taken over by the local doe population, and I'd be willing to bet that if the landowner shoots a mature buck, it's from one of his many stands towards the outside of his parcel, facing outward. The landowner is simply waiting in the evening for a buck to come back onto the parcel towards the huge social area in the middle. The problem? There are only 2 single layers of bedding on either end of the parcel, and if you have a lot of doe family groups in the area, experience has taught me that you shouldn't be surprised if mature bucks don't have much room left for daytime bedding on the property.

Let me start by asking how many of you only have 1 layer of bedding on your property? What about 2? I'm going to discuss how you can position does within narrow areas on your property, how you can keep them there, and how that leaves the bulk of the parcel available for the local mature buck population. As I mentioned before, "Ladies First," and I hope that by the end of this discussion you can see both how and why.

The Concept of Bedding Layers

What I have been able to recognize across the whitetail states that I have explored both for myself and my clients, is that it's often fairly easy to identify a pretty well defined pattern of bedding for both does and bucks. This pattern starts with a major food source, and when doe family groups have adequate bedding nearby, they often will bed very close to that food source, and often within the food source itself if enough cover is present. I call this the 1st layer of bedding. Depending on the deer densities within your area, it may be common that another 2nd layer of bedding is taken over by the local doe family groups as well. When the various layers of bedding are separate and defined, you will most likely recognize that with a little scouting within your favorite hunting grounds, that mature bucks will often be found within the 3rd or 4th layer of bedding. How do you recognize this? Individual beds and concentrated rubbing activity are major clues, and this is one of my favorite locations to scout for and identify for clients when I visit their parcels.

I'm going to keep referring to the previously described 80-acre example so that I can attempt to hammer home this concept. It could be that a major food source is on the west side, the east side, or in this case in the middle, and it could be that you don't have a nearby food source of any kind. But in the example used for this chapter, you need to pull those does away from the side and towards the middle. The first place I'd start is in that giant food plot. There is no reason that you can't have at least a doe family group or two bedding right out in the middle of the food. In this case I'd recommend a few 1/8th acre to ¼ acre islands of cover with a mix of conifers towards the center, shrubs towards the outside - all surrounded by native grasses or native regeneration to, in effect, "screen" the entire bedding pocket. By doing this you can possibly house multiple doe family groups right in the heart of your property. But it doesn't end there!

The next step is to screen the entire perimeter of the food plot... native grasses, shrubs, conifers...feel free to use your imagination. By doing this you hide deer in the woods from the plot, and deer in the plot from the woods. By offering solid pockets of cover within the plot itself, as well as offering that layer of cover surrounding the outside, you will begin to lower the overall stress level within and surrounding the entire food source because deer are hidden from each other, as well as from YOU. Deer will begin to feel more comfortable during the daylight hours using the food source, and deer will also use that plot many hours earlier within the day because they are bedding right next to the food source. It's now time to start your next bedding layer.

Behind that perimeter layer of bedding surrounding the plot, you have now set yourself up for a GREAT 2nd layer of bedding... and I say "2nd layer," because the first layer is within the plot itself by installing the bedding pockets. I'd concentrate on the length of the surrounding perimeter and work on that first 50' of hardwoods. Whether it be an aggressive timber harvest, a complete knock-down mess, carefully constructed and scattered bedding pockets complete with travel corridors, small individual beds, hinge cuts, and conifer plantings...those bedding areas should, for the most part, surround the entire plot. You now have two solid layers of bedding cover, and you can give the doe family groups what they want, which is adequate and scattered bedding opportunity as close to the food source as possible. Within and surrounding a 10-acre food plot (now 8.5 acres after devoting some of the open space to bedding cover), you have the ability to position LOTS of doe family groups. However, some of those does just might have a bad attitude and desire a little more solitude.

Heading into the interior of the woods on either side of the large plot, look for the best potential bedding opportunities. Slight elevation changes, points, inside benches towards the tops of ridges, and higher timber stem, counts per acre areas, all have potential. "Cherry Pick", the best spots at least 50-100' past the bedding layer that surrounds the plot. At this point in your improvements, you now have the potential of THREE layers of bedding cover, which is more than adequate on most parcels to house the majority of all doe family groups that are relating to a strong and consistent food source. Better yet, if you do the math, you've now used 3 separate layers of bedding to stack almost the entire doe herd by using the

INTERIOR 30-35 acres of space, including the food plot, instead of the outside 30-35 acres. At this point there has been a huge amount of progress accomplished, but it is STILL not time to focus on those bucks, because now that you have given a place for those does to hang out, you have to keep them happy!

Happy Does Are Here To Stay

Believe it or not, this is the easiest piece of the entire puzzle, and all that you have to do is to keep the food and cover consistent. The food needs to be consistent in quality and attraction, and the cover consistent in quality and security. If those areas remain consistent, then those does remain happy and have no reason to move. There is no place for deer drives, random woods walks, and in-season scouting missions through this property. You want those does to feel full, fat, happy, and secure the entire season.

You've given the doe family groups the interior ½ of your property, you will focus on keeping them happy in their own area of the property, and those doe family groups will have little reason to leave. It's NOW time to focus on the bucks!

Lots Of Room For Bucks

You can now turn those stands around to face into the property, instead of outward, because the exterior ends of the property that once held the only layer of bedding on the parcel, are now the 4th bedding layer moving outwards from the center...on both ends of the parcel! It's also time to "Cherry Pick" again. With enough room to still be able to move around the borders of your parcel without spooking deer bedded within, look for the best bedding opportunity you can find to enhance. In this manner you have taken a lot of time to locate the doe family groups...and you really don't care exactly where they are. However, you now have the opportunity to locate the mature bucks on the parcel exactly where you want them to be...locations you can count on, hunt between, and even hunt on top of in the morning as bucks return to their beds. My favorite locations start with recognizing multiple doe bedding

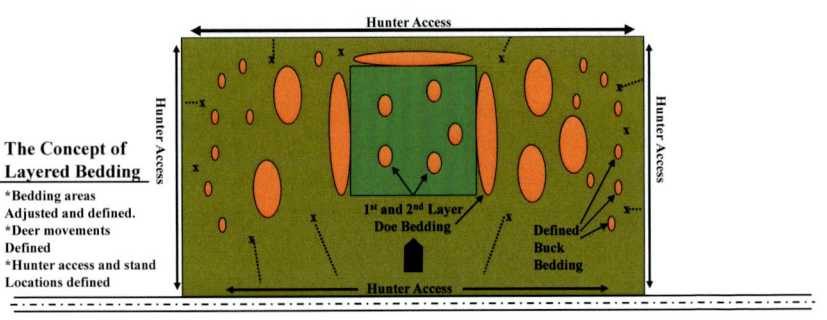

The Concept of Layered Bedding
*Bedding areas Adjusted and defined.
*Deer movements Defined
*Hunter access and stand Locations defined

layers working back from the major food source, and then building the potential buck bedding areas behind those doe family groups. You can also throw in some constructed clear-cut travel corridors to funnel and move deer between bedding areas, parallel to your borders, and eventually towards the interior food source, and you can offer some pretty definitive stand locations to shoot the local mature bucks that now live within your parcel. And while you are at it...WOW, you have no idea how set up those doe family groups are for a late season efficient harvest within and around that large plot when it comes time to thin the herd!

Conclusion

Although some of the details have been left out due to the complexity of all the possible property improvements, the examples provided here should help to illustrate the concept of layered bedding. By establishing multiple layers of bedding locations on your property, the daily movements of bucks and does will become more predictable, and you can maintain a low stress level on your parcel that is easily recognized and attractive to any wandering non-resident mature bucks. Also, by managing the stand of timber between the various beds and bedding layers to promote an increase in habitat diversity, you can drastically improve your parcel's overall deer holding ability. It all starts with the ladies, but in the end there is no reason that you shouldn't be left with the campfire tales about the likes of "Big Moe," "Slick," and "Tallboy."

Chapter 15
HIGH POWERED COOL SEASON BEDDING AREAS

In early December of 2010 my neighbor in Coon Valley, WI, called me with hurried instructions to check out a major game camera company's website to view the "Buck of the Week" photos. "Check out what buck they have pictures of," my neighbor went on to explain. The buck, of course, was one I was personally familiar with. While my lease partner Karl and I were installing treestands and planting our late season food plots throughout the months of spring and summer, we had a local hunter 2 miles away that was getting pictures of this incredible 5-year-old monarch. June, July, August, and September...the pictures on the game camera website were frequent and extremely impressive! And those pictures were equally impressive when we started getting them in September. The hunter that supplied the summer pictures was pretty fired up...commenting that he hadn't heard of the buck being shot and couldn't wait to get his pictures the following year. Would you like to know what the most impressive photos of the year were? They were of Karl kneeling behind the mature beauty following a successful late October hunt. The 168" giant chose to live in one location for the summer growing season... and then, thankfully, chose to live on another for the fall hunting season.

Great summer food sources were part of the equation for why that particular mature buck chose his summer hangout, but a large part of the equation was a result of completely different bedding habitat needs for the warm season months vs. the cool season months. How is the bedding diversity on your parcel? Do you have a great summer hangout, only to lose mature bucks during the fall to better cool season habitats? I would like you to follow along as I discuss what I feel are the 4 critical components of cool season bedding habitat that I have learned to recognize, seek, and promote throughout the northern 1/2 of the whitetail range as I scout dozens of client "deer woods" each year. Also, I look forward to telling you at the end of this writing, which is my absolute favorite bedding component! Timber regeneration, native grasses or weed growth, various shrub varieties, and a collection of conifer species are included within the 4 habitat types that I have found you need to have on your parcel to achieve the appropriate balance of bedding. Whether it's protection from the elements in the form of shade or canopy, the insulating properties of heavy conifer or grasses, or even the ultimate security for deer while hiding within the high stem counts of hardwood regeneration and shrub plantings, balance is key during the most critical time of the year. And why is that period of time the most critical time of the year? Because you don't want to be the one consistently left at the end of the season looking forward to getting pictures of particular bucks the following year, when those bucks are already dead.

Timber Regeneration

Some of my favorite early hunting year memories are burned into my brain in the form of dozens of rubs scattered across several year old timber cuttings. Of course these were some of my favorite hunting grounds for rabbits and grouse as well, but in these locations many forms of wildlife flourished, including deer. And who can blame them? High stem counts per acre of young saplings equal both great cover...AND great food. What a combination!

Personal Favorites

Red Maple, Box Elder, and Aspen all offer an incredible combination of predictably explosive growth with a high level of food value. Red maple will produce succulent shoots of new growth around the stumps of fresh timber harvests, and along the sides of smaller diameter trees that have been hinge-cut to be used to create bedding canopy cover and tunneled sneak trails for secure daytime bedding or travel patterns. Box elder trees are one of the quickest growing and most prolific forms of fencerow and wood line screening cover trees, while aspen clearcuts can produce over 8000 shoots per acre of quick growing wildlife food and cover.

Regeneration Habitat Creations

An effective stand of any daytime bedding cover always starts with making the exterior screened so that the deer bedding within can't see out while you move about your parcel or access stand locations. You will see that diversity is the overall theme of this article, and my favorite hardwood regenerations include the same! Although you may have a completely different variety of timber species in your neck of the woods, the concepts should still be the same. I can picture many woodlots that include aspen and red maple interiors, with box elders towards an ag or field edge along the outside. Box elders usually tip towards the outside of a woodlot while attempting to collect any amount of extra sunlight they can. While those tendencies of crooked, angled, and multi-trunked growth patterns leave little to no timber value to harvest, those same attributes can produce a tangled mess of potential screening cover. Simply take your chainsaw and cut into the backside of the tree at a safe working height, and allow the trunk to tip to the opposite side, towards the direction the trunk is leaning. When the tree starts to tip, you should cease cutting to avoid cutting the outer cambium layer of the tree so that the tree continues to be connected to its lifeline of roots. Box Elder trees are just one of the many species of trees that will continue to flourish even when 75% or more of the diameter of the tree has been cut to create "hinge cuts" to produce an elevated horizontal structure of deer screens, canopied bedding opportunity, and tunneled sneak trails for deer. It's not uncommon to experience up to 8' of new growth out of the side of a spring-cut box elder tree, and by continuing to cut each year, that tangled mess of new growth and old, will create an almost impenetrable fortress of exterior screening cover.

    The next step I like to take in a situation like this is to identify all of the harvestable maple within the stand, as well as every aspen 6" in diameter and larger. Whether you can find a use for yourself or from a timber harvester to remove the cut timber, the point is to cut the trees down to reduce the canopy of sunlight robbing trunks, branches, and leaves, to a minimum of 50% or more. This will allow for optimum regeneration. Red maple shoots will take off from the cut trunks, and aspen will explode into the sun-filled forest floor with 1000s of shoots of new growth taking off from the expansive lateral root system of the cut mature trees. At this time you can use the 2-6" diameter red maples for hinge cuttings and 2" diameter trees and less for bedding area tie-downs over small, dry, level platforms of potential deer beds. "Tie downs" are easy to complete by using braided duck decoy cord to secure young growth to hinged or cut debris to form "living bushes" of chest high browse and canopied bedding cover. Tie downs are great additions to created deer travel corridors through thick growth or cuttings by forming a "sneak tunnel" of deer trails complete with canopy and browse by tying two or more small saplings from either side of deer trails at chest level, directly over the trail. If large trunks and tops are left in the woods...the more the merrier, to equal horizontal bedding cover and "bridging" material to hinge or tie smaller trees to. Keeping the cover suspended to form canopies and living bushes for deer to move under and through is a highly attractive form of bedding habitat that further hides deer herds on the inside of woodlots, from both you...and other deer.

    When you are finished with a stand of timber similar to this, you can offer a bedding area secured on the outside with high quality regeneration species used to screen and protect the woodlot from your movements, as well as a diverse mix of various types of timber regeneration on the inside, to offer a variety of quality bedding habit in the form of canopy, food, horizontal cover, and high stem counts per acre. An added tip; after you have completed your timber cuttings, don't forget to further define those bedding areas by adding shade tolerant conifers, such as White Spruce or White Pine in northern settings.

Grasses and Native Weed Growth

As a 17 year old in 1987 I experienced one of my most memorable hunts, and I was only the observer. While my brother and I were walking along an overgrown fence row that connected a 5 woodlot ½ mile from the farmhouse, we spotted a doe and fawn feeding within the overgrown hay field only 100 yards away. The deer were settled within a mix of native grasses, golden rod, and most likely a little ragweed, while I told my 15-year-old brother that he should try a stalk on the unsuspecting pair. Maybe it was because I didn't think it was possible and I didn't want to bother…or maybe it was a sliver of "brotherly love," but regardless, Kevin crouched down and attempted to crawl within bow range. I think we must have felt like "pros" 25 years ago, because we coordinated hand signals for when it was safe to move or not, picked a spot in the field for him to get to for a shot, and to our amazement it worked! Kevin used the cover of the grasses and weeds to literally crawl across 80 yards of "cover" to get to within 20 yards. It was at that time our lack of experience showed in that Kevin got into position, rose up for the shot…and missed! And I can say "our lack of experience" because with only a couple of years of hunting under both of our belts, it was likely I would have done the same. It was a great time hunting a long time ago as well as an early lesson in the value of grasses and weeds for feeding deer, hiding deer, and making deer feel safe while you access your stand locations and move about your property.

Personal Favorites

Is switch grass great? Sure. Big Blue Stem, Little Blue Stem, and Indian Grass? Sure! But so is the native early successional growth of overgrown ag fields, including ragweed, goldenrod, briars, thistle, and other native species. And don't underestimate the power of annual varieties like Egyptian Wheat that has the potential to grow quickly, thick, and 10' tall or more. By now you can probably recognize the common theme of overall "Diversity," and it truly is the key to any successful bedding habitat.

Grass Habitat Creations

If your ag field grows a "mess" of diversity that reaches chest high and has the ability to effectively hide a small daytime deer herd...outstanding, that may be all that you need! However, there is often a need for plantings including a host of native grass varieties. Large plantings of native grasses, including the likes of Switch grass, Big Blue Stem, Little Blue Stem, and Indian Grass, can be daytime magnets for deer herds during portions of the hunting season; and I've personally enjoyed picking off does with a rifle at long distances while targeting doe family groups that were attracted to the thermal properties of native grass fields flanked by large wind blocking ridges and timber lines during bitter December temperatures.

And what about the power of Egyptian Wheat? During the last couple of years my clients have enjoyed using the variety to screen bedding areas, hide food sources, and to offer secure travel corridors for both deer and hunters. A 10' wide strip broadcasted at 15-20 lbs per acre, will offer a solid screen 8-10' high or more, that allows a hunter to move about the outside of the planting with the correct wind and lack of noise, completely undetected. Need to hide deer within food sources or future grass bedding areas until more permanent screenings take over in the form of grasses, bushes, or conifers? Egyptian wheat is a superb option with only a 110 day growing season and a solid wall of cover within a very short period of time.

When Kevin and I were just teenagers hunting on our own from a non-hunting family, we had no idea what we were doing, no idea of the power of grasses, weeds, and briars, or frankly how to plan for using it to our advantage. However, for a brief period of time on a sunny afternoon near the Cass City River in lower MI, hunting lessons were learned through an overgrown field, a couple of deer, and an 80 yard stalk that was successful despite the lost arrow.

Shrubs

"Wildlife Plantings" was the section in the Conservation District tree planting order guide, and it included some awesome shrub varieties of Dogwood, Nannyberry, Hazelnut, and Elderberry. A friend of mine was salivating at the prospect of a 10-acre field full of various shrubs to house small game, birds, and deer. Berries, cover, nesting and escape cover…a 10-acre field of shrubs can be a true sanctuary for many varieties of wildlife. He signed up for a cost share assistance program, and a few months later the plantings were in the ground. Sounds like a story with a very successful ending…right? Well, it could have been except for the fact that often "Wildlife Plantings" should be more correctly labeled as "Deer Food," as every young shrub variety was browsed enough so that not 1 plant remained within 2 years. So, which is the best shrub to plant? Simply, the one that will grow! Now that is not to say that you don't plant some of your favorite varieties with tree tubes, shelters, and cages, but again, MAKE SURE that they have a chance to grow, because some of the best shrub plantings also make great deer food.

Personal Favorites

The list is extremely short of browse resistant varieties you may choose to use, so I suggest you use a base of browse resistant shrubs, coupled with a variety of shelter protected varieties, to offer the diversity needed to be consistent with good deer bedding habitat. Speckled alder is a great shrub that grows to a 12' x 12' extremely thick mound of quality habitat, and is not readily consumed by deer even in high population areas. Honeysuckle is another planting that actually tolerates a fair amount of browsing pressure and can also be used for tight-spaced plantings for access and screening cover. There may also be other shrub varieties that you find on your parcel that seem to flourish and provide excellent cover, and if so…use them to your advantage. Often "local" varieties will be your #1 choice.

Shrub Habitat Creations

To me there is nothing more natural than grouping shrubs within clumps, surrounded by native grasses or early successional growth. Avoid rowed plantings in order to produce a more natural, low stress environment for all animal species, including deer. Rowed plantings of any tree or shrub plantings are efficient for large-scale efforts, but at the same time create a very unnatural setting for wildlife. As a side note, I often recommend 3-4 rows of conifer for property border access routes to offer great screening for hunter access, with a low probability of potential deer bedding cover compared to staggered or irregular creations. Plantings of 10-12 shrubs, with the opportunity to hollow out portions facing the interior of the grouping and hide deer within, is a highly effective practice. Using existing plantings to form small bedding pockets is a very good practice that can substantially increase bedding opportunities on your parcel this year!

Shrub creations and plantings can be planted or manipulated into high quality bedding opportunities that are hidden, offer a food component, and provide nesting and escape cover for many wildlife species. However, what is the most important aspect of the plantings? Just make sure they become wildlife cover, and not wildlife food!

Conifers

Some of the coldest, darkest, deer-less portions of deer habitat I have walked through have been within stands of conifer, including mature white cedar, red cedar, and various spruces. On the other hand some of the most deer-filled portions of habitat have been just the same! It's often feast or famine with solid plantings of conifers, and if you rely on them for the bulk of the bedding cover on your property, you may really be limiting yourself. I had a forester I met in the Midwest who share with me that he found over 50 sheds within his food plot, adjacent to his large planting of red cedar in late spring. I assumed that meant that he had a great deer herd during the hunting season and probably shot some giants! But nope...he told me he had very few bucks during the season, and they only moved in for the food and cover during the months of winter. He had a GREAT bedding area for a very limited portion of the year due to the complete lack of diversity within his bedding habitat.

Personal Favorites

Red pines and other quick growing conifers can be great for producing 6-8' ground cover within 5 years, and when a tight spacing of 5' or less is used, a solid visual barrier can be produced fairly quickly. Red pines lose their lower branches with age, so white pines can be a complement or even replacement to red pine, and White or Norway spruce can produce a solid wall of branches all the way to the ground for 100 years or more. Red cedar can be established on very poor soil types and they can be a great addition to steep ridges or points within stands of hardwoods where soil types may be less than desirable and timber production poor. Northern White Cedar is an incredible winter habitat, but is very difficult to establish due to temperamental soil requirements and the risk of over-browsing.

Conifer Habitat Creations

Similar to various shrub varieties, conifers can be great additions to your parcel when planted in clumps of 10-20' in diameter or less. Avoid rows for a more natural and low stress environment, and small openings within your planted clumps are great to offer for an increase in diversity of habitat within pretty tight quarters.

I often work with landowners who have already established 5-10 acres of rowed conifer plantings or more through some type of state or federally assisted cost share program. Although this isn't necessarily ideal year round whitetail bedding cover, it can be improved! I like to take a 20' wide by 40-50' long block of plantings and completely remove or harvest the conifer species. Early successional growth can be allowed to take over, shrubs can be planted, and even temporary bedding grass combos can be planted within while taking advantage of increased amounts of sunlight. I like irregular shaped openings running mostly north and south, to take advantage of the high midday sun for improved growing conditions. In the future, various trees surrounding your bedding openings can be harvested to maintain an open canopy, with plenty of sunlight hitting your bedding pockets to continue the diversity of habitat growing within. What I really like with this type of creation is that you can specifically dictate exactly where the deer will be bedding within an entire stand of conifer plantings, and that can be a great advantage for your hunting efforts.

One of my most memorable and effective bedding area improvements started by carving out holes within small islands of conifer surrounded by swamp and marsh in MI's Upper Peninsula back in 2001. Those small islands of cover were located well, but literally too thick for anything but small game and birds. By cutting and removing limbs chest high and lower on the inside of the small 1/8 acre to ¼ acre stands of white cedar, balsam fir, and white spruce to create a pattern of small rooms, deer would immediately take over...most often within several weeks. "Rooms" the size of a pick-up bed or small living room are perfect for housing bedded deer of all ages and sex, and it's important to create a network of trails in and out of each pocket to produce a "maze and pocket" effect. For the past 11 years I have applied that same "Maze and Pocket" concept to clumps of bushes, tangled hardwood cuttings and regeneration, as well as open grass areas and early successional growth with similar results. Same concept...different habitats.

I would love to get a chance to work on the Midwest forester's property, and the overall theme would be no different than this article...Diversity is key!

CONCLUSION

Karl's buck was a beauty and is in our top 3 for age and size out of the couple of dozen bucks shot on our lease property over the past 11 years. With 1000s of game camera photos throughout the last several years, we have seen the same thing year after year; about 2/3rds of our bucks that visit our property regularly throughout the season do not typically appear until AFTER the season starts. We typically have between 8 and 12 bucks of 4 years old or older to consistently target during the hunting season, and only a fraction of those are present during the months of spring and summer. We have good cool-season food sources which are critical, and so do some of our neighbors, but the big difference between our property and some of the summer mature buck hangouts, is the type of bedding cover we have, vs. theirs. Summer time mature bucks love shade, airflow, and the cooler temps of the tall canopy of open hardwoods adjacent to lush summer food sources of beans and alfalfa. We just don't have either of those ingredients on our parcel, but is it really cause for concern? I don't think so. We get to house a very sizeable buck herd on our 180-acres that offers protection, food, and quality cover throughout the majority of fall and well into the winter months. By collecting bucks during that time we get to offer them quality cool-season annual forages during a period of very little in the whitetail woods, we are able to promote a higher age structures of bucks, and we have the ability to improve sex ratios. And the fun part about hunting? We get to shoot does at will when needed for the health of the herd, and specifically target the same mature bucks every year no matter where they live during the months of spring and summer. This year we will get a chance at our first 7 year old, following a great picture of him on Valentine's Day of this year... the latest date we have ever snapped a photo of him. In his case we have protected him because I have missed...but that's another chapter altogether!

And what is my all-time favorite bedding habitat component? All of them! Diversity is key, and when you combine small pockets of conifer surrounded by shrubs and native grasses or early successional growth, with adjacent timber regeneration creations, the possibilities are endless. Bedding diversity will provide protection from the elements in the form of shade or canopy, insulating properties in the form of heavy conifer or grasses, and the ultimate level of security for deer while they seek the daytime comfort within high stem counts of hardwood regeneration and shrub plantings. For a quick assessment of your bedding cover, take a look at the overall height. If the top of your bedding cover is all the same, whether it be native grass, conifer, hardwoods, or even shrubs, your bedding cover most likely lacks diversity. If the upper height of your bedding cover rises up and down like the outline of the big buck county bluffs of the Mighty Mississippi, then you are on the right track! Ok maybe not that high, but you can get the picture. Diversity is key, and it's key for you being the one getting the hunting season pictures of that monster you watched all summer long while you attract, hold, hunt, and even promote him to the next age class.

Chapter 16

BALANCE DIAGNOSIS OF FOOD AND COVER

I love to diagnose deer parcels! Every parcel in every region, every state, every county and even in the same "neighborhood," have a unique set of variables that form a puzzle of habitat and hunting prescriptions for success. In short, one of the coolest things about walking dozens of parcels each year is to be able to explore and scout what exactly the deer are doing on each parcel. Where the local deer herd beds, eats, and travels on your parcel is cool enough...but unraveling the clues that indicate when the deer are on a parcel during the year, why they are there at that time, what sex or age of deer is using the parcel, and even why they are not there...is where the true fun begins. I had a MN client tell me during a follow-up call in the spring of 2012, "you could sure tell you had fun doing what you did on my property," and he was right! To me, the beauty of what makes every whitetail property "fun," is that they are all different...every one of them.

I can go into a host of various types of diagnosis for whitetail parcels with the subtitles of "Access", "Exterior Hunting Pressure", "Stand Locations", "Water", and several more...but one of the biggest balancing acts across the whitetail range lies in the prescription of "Food and Cover." In a nutshell, if you have too much cover, deer will often leave during critical times of the hunting season to find food, and if you have too much food, deer will often leave during critical times of the hunting season to find cover. Sound confusing? Well it isn't, if you follow along on the thought process of food/cover diagnosis, prescription, and location for success.

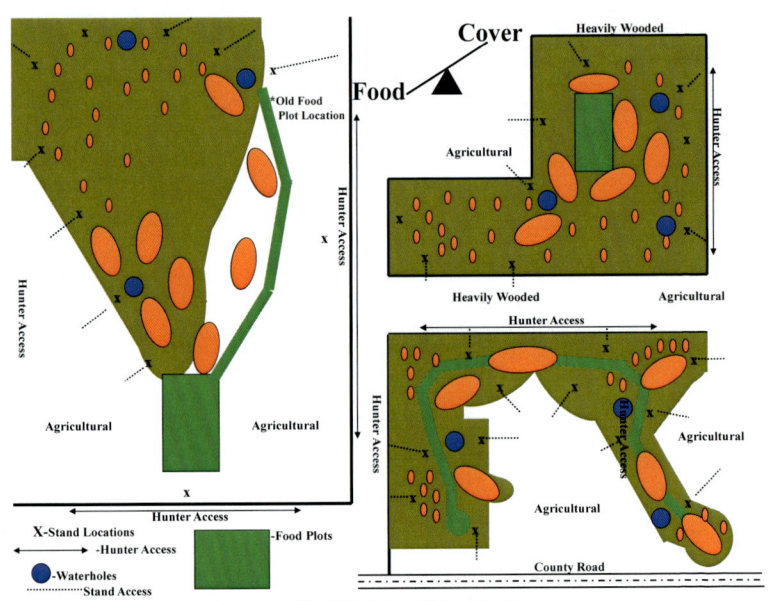

Diagnosis #1, Too Much Cover

Description of Parcel: The parcel in the upper right hand corner is located within a mixed ag region of large ag fields, woodlots, and small rural housing developments. Large ag fields sprawl to the west and northwest of the parcel, as well as to the southeast, with a small country residential development that once was additional ag land. The parcel contains an explosion of young growth after logging activities within the last 10 years, and is combined with a gentle westerly facing slope on the west side of the parcel, mixed with red cedar and low brush.

Diagnosis:

*The diagnosis of "too much cover" is due to the fact that cover parcels are also available on the north and south borders of the parcel.

*Great ag land is plentiful, but quality hunting season food sources are lacking.

It is key to understand that there is a vast difference between great ag land filled with crops of soybeans, corn, and hay...and great HUNTING SEASON food sources. The two are not 1 in the same.

*Without the availability of quality hunting season forages the parcel lacks both attraction and definition of movement, resulting in an overall theme of chaotic and undefined deer movements on both the subject parcel and those that surround.

*Undefined deer movements equal a much higher likelihood of spooking deer, and the lack of a consistent food source for attraction leaves the landowner hoping to catch a fleeing deer, or possibly a cruising mature buck traveling through the parcel in search of a doe.

*A typical parcel such as this, may offer good pre-season observations of mature bucks as they dine within the adjacent ag lands, but at the same time, an ever decreasing buck observation rate as the ag land food sources dwindle. With the shrinking food sources, the bulk of the deer herd centers their attention on neighboring hunting season food sources of late standing crops or food plots.

*In the field, observations reveal passing/traveling mature buck signs and a lack of consistent focus for daytime bedding use or mature buck daytime use in general.

Prescription for Success

*Food. By offering a large food source within an existing centrally located open field and a smaller northerly food source against the landowners adjacent "leased land," the landowner can then attempt to house doe family groups between the two food sources.

*The attraction and resulting higher level of deer stress/usage will create a very high center of doe family group usage on the northern 1/2 of the parcel...while creating a lower level of stress on the southern 1/2 of the parcel.

*By using food to create varying levels of stress within the parcel boundaries, bedding areas can then be enhanced and created for both mature buck and doe family group bedding.

*Outside travel corridors running easterly/westerly towards the northeast corner as well as close to the southern border, can be created to offer hunting opportunities while mature bucks cruise the outside downwind edge of the cover while scent-checking the interior improvements of food or cover.

*By using food on this parcel, the parcel then receives "definition." Definition of food source, definition of doe bedding, definition of buck bedding, and finally definition of deer travel patterns.

*"Definition" equals attraction, holding ability, and efficiency in hunting opportunity. By promoting definition in the overall deer use of the parcel, even a small parcel of less than 40 acres of cover, such as the subject parcel, can significantly reduce the overall level of stress and chaos within the entire neighborhood. By following a system of balance and definition the landowner will have the ability to literally shape the quality level of the entire deer herd within the area because of the influence the parcel can have over the protection of young bucks, the ability to control doe numbers, and the opportunity to attract, hold and harvest mature bucks during the hunting season.

Diagnosis #2, Too Much Food

Description of Parcel: The parcel located in the upper left corner is an exceptional parcel located within a rural ag setting of 100' elevation changes, mixed habitat types, and a solid local buck age structure. A large portion of wooded cover extends north of the subject parcel through rolling and broken ridges, flanked by easterly and westerly sprawling ag fields within the lower elevations. The 57-acre subject parcel features a central ridge system running east/west on the north side, with a spur of the ridge filled with a diversity of cover jutting south to form a high "T" protruding into the ag fields below.

Diagnosis:
*The label of "Too much Food" in some respects is due largely to the location of that food. The food is tucked into the inside corner of the "T" of the right side of the ridge system, which is in the northeast corner of the property.

*Due to the location of the food, the landowner can't access the parcel along the east edge without spooking feeding deer while he is getting in and out of potential stand locations to take advantage of the dominant westerly wind patterns.

*The location of the food is flanked by the long narrow ridge system that features a very shallow Depth of Cover located between the food source edge and the outer edge of the cover.

*By placing the food source along the narrow side of the ridge cover, doe family groups take over the adjacent food source bedding cover, and there is little, to no Depth of Cover to house mature bucks behind the typical doe family group bedding locations.

Prescription for Success:

*Depth of Cover. By using the concept of Depth of Cover as discussed in a previous chapter, I hope that you can begin to see how this parcel can be substantially improved by simply moving the food source to the south end of the long, narrow ridge of cover. Instead of the cover being 100 yards deep at best, it can quickly be changed to several hundred yards of depth for a maximum Depth of Cover Efficiency Percentage.

*Another positive aspect of the change in food source location, is the creation of more cover. By replacing the food source with cover, a much broader area of secure daytime bedding cover can be created within a fairly remote area of the property. Currently the landowner has planted various types of conifers and shrubs to surround the food plots that can be relocated, setting up a great opportunity to replace lush green forages with bedding whitetails. By hiding deer within the new daytime bedding cover, it will aid the landowner in accessing the parcel along the east property line, keeping the stress level of the parcel low, and the options for access high.

Diagnosis #3, Too Little Cover and Food

Description of Parcel: The parcel in the lower right corner has the ability to one day be an exceptional whitetail property due to its sprawling, long lines of potential cover mixed with food. Currently, though, the long slender fingered ridges featuring mature hardwoods, has little to no food or cover value. The parcel is deceiving because the bulk of the hardwoods is surrounded by expansive ag fields to the north, west, south, and east, giving it the illusion of "plenty of food." However, when the beans turn brown in early September, and the corn is picked in October, there is very little food left for any deer that could potentially be housed on the parcel. Those long fingers of cover that would otherwise be a substantial blessing to this potential whitetail hotspot, are instead a major hindrance to reaching the parcel's full potential. Without food, there is little reason for doe family groups to stay as the crops begin to be harvested, and even less of a reason for mature bucks to call this type of habitat home during the most critical periods of hunting season. Even the best of potential locations cannot come close to their highest possible level of success when both hunting season food sources and quality cover is lacking.

Diagnosis:
*A great piece of information that the landowner shared with me while we were scouting his land was that as the season

progressed, there were fewer and fewer opportunities for mature bucks, and the overall deer numbers quickly faded as gun season approached. The best gun season and later hunting parcels I have experienced all have two things in common: Great hunting season food sources, and great hunting season bedding cover. *When the hunting season sightings are decreasing instead of increasing, that fact carries with it a large clue into the diagnosis of the parcel.

*Quality bedding cover alone at this time of the year is not enough, with the exception of being within the smallest of cover-starved ag regions, but even then, deer will leave that cover to find quality food sources if available. And it's no different with great food sources that are not supported by enough quality cover. When the pressure is on and deer stress levels are rising, those open, mature hardwoods that housed significant deer numbers during the early fall, can be completely devoid of deer even when fall food sources are outstanding. When the cover is bare, and those quality food sources on your parcel begin to feature nocturnal use only, it's not because the deer are nocturnal; instead, it's because you have a nocturnal parcel.

*Without quality hunting season food or cover sources, the parcel in the lower right hand corner of the drawing unfortunately cannot even be considered a nocturnal parcel, as deer have little to no reason to return unless they are heavily pressured to do so.

Prescription for Success:

*Using the incredible length of cover that this parcel has available, a focus of food and cover improvements can be used to substantially increase the potential of Whitetail Success. Unfortunately, little to no ag land can be used for food or cover, with the exception of a small connection of cover to be created within the most northerly portion of the farmland, to connect to the east and west woodlots.

*Large destination food sources are not an option for several reasons, including the overall amount of work, time, and expense to do so. However, the parcel is blessed with an outstanding inner road system that snakes along the 3 main ridge lines the parcel features. 2 lengths of food, covering several hundred yards each, and a width of 20' or less, can be installed to fill the food source vacancy, while the inward facing points and benches can be manipulated to provide dozens of quality bedding areas that are hidden and away from the view of hunter access.

*The long ridgelines are perfect for providing outstanding hunter access! With improvements, including food sources, kept primarily to the opposite side of the ridge from hunter access, hunters can enjoy some superb "deer-less" access points. Stand locations alongside the lengthy narrow food plots for afternoon sits, or on the backside of improved bedding locations during morning sits, give the landowners a great variety of potential stand locations for evening or morning hunting, as well as early, rut, and late season sits.

*Clear-cut travel corridors can be used to hide deer while traveling from food sources and bedding locations, and offer outstanding locations to catch rut-cruising mature bucks.

*By using less than 10% of the total amount of available timbered habitat for bedding areas, food sources, and travel corridors, the landowner can finally attain the maximum potential of Whitetail Success.

Conclusion

Asking the question of which is the most important, "Food or Cover," is not much different than searching for the answer to an age old question of which came first, the "chicken or the egg?" As discussed in an article featured in Quality Whitetails several years ago my wife and I, in 1995, were able to buy 37 acres of mostly pastured, river-bottom land in southern MI, with an extremely low

% of cover. No buck sign was present, but within 2 years, 7 different bucks were able to be passed on during the first 7 sits of the year after planting 9000 trees by hand, allowing the browsed out habitat to regenerate, and installing less than 2 acres of food plots. In 2004 I was honored with the 2004 Al Brother's Deer Manager of the Year Award for taking a 120-Acre tract in MI's Upper Peninsula and building a deer herd consisting of various age classes of bucks, good sex ratios, and a population in balance with the habitat. All of that was accomplished by simply adding several acres of quality food sources, practicing appropriate harvest objectives, and allowing the property to collect deer during the hunting season through low-impact hunting methods, including "Predatory Access." 400 miles apart, those two parcels of mine were drastically different in habitat, deer herds, hunting pressure, and location, but just like the 3 parcels detailed within this chapter, they also varied greatly in their balance of food or cover. However, unlike those parcels of mine that are 400 miles apart, the parcels detailed within this chapter were less than 20 miles apart. Even within the same neighborhood, a parcel's needs can vary greatly, so take some time to attempt to diagnose your hunting land's balance of food and cover Balance of Food and Cover to achieve your ultimate level of whitetail success!

Wisconsin Archery Bucks

Chapter 17

BUILDING PART TIME DEER HERDS

"Healthy" dead bucks don't grow either! Just imagine your dreams for that handsome looking 2-year 10 old point that has been feeding in your alfalfa field all summer. He is with a little "brat pack" of 2 other young bucks that you just know are going to be some real studs in the coming years. Those little buddies love to hang out all day under the cool overstory of the open mature hardwoods within your woodlot. The trio have been dining first on your clover in May, and then all summer long on the lush alfalfa that is power-packed with both nutrition and attraction. Larger antlers, higher body weights, and overall health have you beaming with pride at the potential. As the summer progresses into mid-September the boys begin to test each other while sparring lightly with their 2nd set of hard antlers. The first frost of October comes around and the leaves trade their slick green coats of summer for their vibrant shades of fall. The trio becomes 2, and then 1, as they move off to find their own hunting season hangouts, but you get some trail cam photos of them as they still relate to the summer comfort you provided. During the season you get a few glimpses of the trio, and each time you can't wait to see them the following year. Then, the "horror" begins as first one of the nice little 8 points falls to a neighbor a mile away, then the other 8 point, and finally the 10 point ends up falling in line for a trip to another neighbor's wall. To add insult to injury, everyone commented on how heavy they were for 2 year olds-Good Job!

Now of course bucks love to wander, especially during the rut. But at the same time they will wander for other reasons, too; namely food and security cover. In this article I'm going to talk about how your hunting season focus of nutritional attraction can play a critical role in your efforts to ultimately experience a quality herd on your parcel. I will discuss what type of plantings you may want to consider, when to plant them, and strategically, how your plantings can make or break not only your management efforts, but your level of hunting season success as well. On small parcels you need to move away from the thought that you can take care of the local deer herd for 12 months out of the year. If you focus first on the 3 most critical months and do your best to offer as high of quality habitat improvements that you can at that time of the year, you are better off than going ½ way for the entire rest of the year. It's called managing and hunting a "Part-time Deer Herd" and as long as you hit those 3 critical months, your ability to experience a quality herd can be exceptional.

When to Peak

In the Midwest, without a doubt, your food sources should be at the highest level they can be in November. Think November first, and then work out to the surrounding months. Consider that deer throughout the Midwest and most northern areas have several times more quality forage than they can utilize during the summer months. I personally have my doubts that in many Midwest settings you can actually increase the overall quality and nutrition enough to notice a change in the local deer herd except in the poorest of conditions. On top of that, it never bothered me if my neighbors were taking care of the deer all summer long that I'm hunting in Oct/Nov/Dec. I'd hate to offer food in June/July/August at the expense of the more critical period of hunting season.

What to Plant

In order to know what to plant, you have to think about what local forages can really give you the most bang for your buck in November. In my own personal Midwest food plot plantings in MN, WI, and both northern and southern MI, it has been tough to beat the rotated forages of brassicas and grains. Brassica combinations including forage soybeans, buckwheat, and peas can really give your planting a boost, and I've always liked a mix of grains including oats, wheat, and winter rye. Both the grains AND the brassicas offer a considerable amount of attraction and nutrition in November, especially when compared to what the local habitat or ag fields have to offer at the time.

Something to ponder..."Is it better to offer a forage that is 5/10 on the nutritional scale at a time when the local habitat and ag fields are 2/10?....or to offer a forage that is 10/10 at a time when the local habitat and ag fields are also at 10/10? Often it's not the overall quality of the forage that will be the key to your success but the difference in quality between that forage and the local habitat at the time of the forages usage.

Think November when choosing your forages, surrounded by October and December, and finally September and January wrapping it all up. If you can start your forages in September, get them to come together in November, and then at least let them slowly diminish into the end of January, you have just accomplished an incredible task. Best of all, if grains were used within your equation, then you just hit a period of time prior to spring green-up that is rarely touched, providing an adequate green forage 2-4 weeks prior to when any clover fields have awakened from their long winter naps.

Providing forages that are available in August or at the very latest in September, is important because it begins the pattern of use on your food sources. It is important to offer the consistent variety of forage on EVERY food plot, so that the chain of movements and use can be initiated early. Then when October rolls around the deer have been following the same pattern for several weeks and by the time the November offerings become attractive it's a natural progression for the deer to move over a few feet and continue to move and feed. By offering the consistency in attraction and variety throughout November, TOGETHER with daytime bedding security, I have found deer to heavily gravitate to this type of setting. If your food continues throughout December get ready for late season muzzleloader and archery seasons! Food is king during the late hunting season and if you offer quality cool-season cover too... WOW-enjoy! And finally, when quality food carries the local deer herd through January they are well on their way to enjoying an energy boost within the dead of winter that will reap a great head start of rewards for the following summer's growing season.

The timing of when various forages are available, should determine exactly what you plant. To many times the ultimate level of nutrition receives an unwarranted focus, instead of when your local deer herd needs the forage based on your management objectives. What I like to do is to offer 2 different combinations of plantings that target 4 critical periods of forage needs, including: Pre-season (Augusts/September), in-season (Oct-Dec), post-season (Jan-March) and pre-spring green-up (April). Taking a look at the table below, I have put together a list of various popular deer forages, and the typical window of use I have experienced that deer utilize the most. An example of the timing I look for in a couple of fairly easy plantings would be a brassica/soybean combo planted around 8/1 that targets the period of August-March, and a grain/pea combo planted around 9/1 that target August to December, and again in April. I like to plant those two plantings side by side, and expect to enjoy a variety of "peaks" during an overall window of use covering several months.

Midwest Forage Window Peaks of Typical Use:
    1. Clover…..September/October
    2. Alfalfa…..July/August
    3. Brassica…..November/December
    4. Grains…..September to November, April (wheat and rye only)
    5. Peas/Soybeans…..August to October
    6. Buckwheat…..August/September
    7. Chicory'….July/August
    8. Corn…..November-February
    9. Spring Planted Soybeans…..Dec-February

Corn and spring planted soybeans do have their place in the world of food plots, but typically require large amounts of acreage that many deer hunters lack the resources to employ, including myself.

When to Plant

With the exception of corn, so many forages can be planted during the late summer and that is of benefit to you in the form of fresh young growth. Brassicas have about a 12 week maturity so late July plantings in much of the Midwest is appropriate, and I really like to plant grains within 2-4 weeks of the expected first frost. On my SW WI lease that means the forages of brassicas, buckwheat, and soybeans can be planted in late July, and a grain and pea combo can be planted around 9/1. The combinations of soybeans and/or buckwheat within your brassica mix also packs a little more punch during the early season than with brassicas alone.

Rarely do you need to plant during the springtime because outside of planting corn and soybeans, the majority of deer-specific forages can and/or should be planted during the late summer. For example, brassica combinations of rape, turnips and radishes should be planted around August 1st in the north ½ of the country, and grains of wheat, oats or rye do quite well with a target of Labor Day weekend. At the same time, perennials such as clover or chicory do extremely well when combined with brassica or grain plantings during the late summer. Establishing your perennials during the late summer is a great practice that allows the young plants to grab a good foothold at a time when weeds are dying and not thriving, as well as at a time when moisture is typically increasing, instead of decreasing. When combining perennial plantings to cool season annual plantings such as brassicas or grains, let the cool season annual dictate the optimum planting date, and make sure to still plant the recommended amount of perennial seed per acre.

Conclusion

My personal camera observations have always revealed an explosion in buck population within the months of October and November. And I'm not talking about midnight wanderers from 3 miles away; I'm talking about mature bucks that set up shop for 2-3 months with multiple daytime sightings in person and by game camera. By offering great hunting season food and cover, you can end up with a "Part-time" deer herd on your parcel that has the potential for some great hunting season "fun", with the additional benefits of improved sex ratios and buck age structure. Instead of your neighbor congratulating you on how fat the 2 year old buck was that he shot, the better form of compliment a neighbor can give to you is… "Why do you always shoot the mature bucks I feed all summer on my parcel, on your parcel?" Just smile and say, "Thanks for taking care of them for me"! Learn to manage and plan for a part-time deer herd with great hunting season forages, and then expand your efforts if you have the resources. And remember, "Healthy Dead Bucks Don't Grow Either".

Chapter 18

ESTABLISHING PATTERNS OF FOOD PLOT USE

In 2005 I made a major blunder on a very important planting on our WI Lease. It was a brassica planting, and before some of you bemoan brassica plantings, consider it was not the variety of seed that was the problem. On our lease we have an incredible SW leg of a food plot hidden within a "horseshoe shaped" idle ag field flanked by various bedding areas on the sides, as well as the west end. We've harvested quite a few bucks within the area, as well as taken in total, the best collection of mature buck pictures on the property. To say this area of the property is important to us is an understatement...it's "where dreams are made of".

The planting was perfect, the results were outstanding, and in October we were left with a brassica mixture of various seed varieties that totaled 2 acres and over 30" tall. LOTS of food! However, the 550 yards planting, snaking its way along the north side of the slight ridge through the CRP field, was barely getting touched. As the pre-rut approached we were getting worried, but still it was barely touched...just a leaf here, a leaf there, and between that and the problems we were having with daytime temperatures into the 70s, our November rut hunt turned out to be pretty slow. I feel we effectively wrote off that entire area of our property because, instead of maintaining that pattern of feeding in that location of the parcel, we destroyed it and expected the deer to slam into the pattern of the brassicas in late October like they had been there all season...only they hadn't.

It was at this time that the term "Pattern of Use" really began to be cemented into my practices. I'm going to explain to you what a pattern of use is, why it needs to be established, and how it relates to the majority of your management efforts. I don't mind admitting my mistakes, and I've found that the more I've made, the more I've learned. Hopefully you can learn from my mistakes and effectively establish the patterns of use on your parcel that will keep both you and the local deer herd happy throughout ALL of the months of the hunting season.

What is a Pattern of Use?

Many of you have probably seen those fancy food plot chain examples that are, in theory, supposed to move deer from "Point A" to "Point B" through the use of varying quality forages. "In theory" it sounds great! Deer like variety, deer like to move, and deer like to forage while moving...sounds good, right? The problem lies in the fact that certain forages are not attractive during certain times of the hunting season. The above example includes brassicas which typically increase in attraction during the later ½ of November. At the same time, with an early frost alfalfa might have been stemmy, yellow, and dormant a full 2 months earlier. Put the two on adjacent plots you are attempting to encourage the deer to travel through within the "chain" of movement, and you have one giant 2-month-gaping-hole in both attraction and nutrition. The deer will not follow any intended pattern of use in that situation.

Instead, an actual pattern of use in the above scenario, would be to offer both alfalfa and brassica, side by side, in each field; but still, that is only a start. So add some grains, such as wheat or rye, to offer a bridge for the months of usage between the alfalfa and brassicas, and NOW you are establishing a pattern of use, as well as effectively manipulating the deer movements. The variety of forage needs to be in each plot...not in separate plots.

If you expect the deer to use your small hunting plot on the way to a larger food source or bedding area, the pattern should be started early and often, and that goes for any habitat improvement within a line of movement you are attempting to create, including long thin plantings of forages designed to facilitate deer travel. In that case, the variety of forages need to run LENGTHWISE along the planting so that when one forage is more attractive than another, the deer just step over and continue their movements.

Maybe you are attempting to move deer through separated food plots on their way to a larger destination? Make sure those gaps aren't too thin; meaning, a deer has to feel secure enough to travel through the area in both the early AND the late season, which means cover has to be at a premium or you won't be able to facilitate those movements on your parcel.

Why Establish Patterns of Use?

Without effective patterns the local deer herd experiences a chaotic movement in and around your parcel of land. Instead, you want the deer to "flow" through your land, feeling comfortable and having many hours of habitat features and use to work through, so that they spend more time on your property. When the patterns are chaotic the deer simply "jump ship" to other areas that potentially may or may not be on your parcel.

Also, deer patterns of use need to be consistent so that you as a hunter know exactly where to define their travels. The more you can define the deer's daily travel patterns, the easier they are to hunt. At the same time, the more defined the pattern is, the easier it is to keep the deer within that pattern on your property. On a small parcel you simply cannot afford to not establish effective patterns of use on the parcel early and consistently throughout the season.

When those patterns are consistent, the deer tend to feed more efficiently and consistently on your plots as well. For example, the local deer have a hard time adjusting all of their patterns up to a certain date, and feeding on the forage you are offering in early November, just because the lone brassica field suddenly is attractive. In some locals, by the time the brassica is really attractive, the deer are already on to greener pastures and heavy cover, never to return during the winter months. Instead, offer those early season crops such as soybeans planted in late July, buckwheat, and even various grains planted just a few weeks prior to the season, within the same plot, running lengthwise the way you want the deer to travel.

How Does a Pattern of Use Relate to Your Goals?

Simply, without consistency in both food and cover throughout the season, the deer will attempt to find that consistency somewhere else. Gaps in food and gaps in cover all add up to chaotic movements in and out of your parcel. Buck age structure is affected because you lose a higher % of those bucks to your neighbors, while at the same time you fail to attract your potential of mature bucks during the season, mainly because there are times when deer just don't have much of a reason to re-locate to your parcel during mid-season. As far as your hunting efforts, it's not out of the question to consistently be the one in your neighborhood to shoot the majority of the mature bucks. When your parcel features a high level of security and quality food source throughout the entire season, you can experience a very high level of success IF your mature buck hunting tactics are ready for the challenge...but that is another article topic!

Conclusion

I've learned a lot since that 2005 season blunder, and I should have known better at the time. The plot was a GREAT one...just a very bad application. Through consistency of quality you have the ability to collect deer as the season progresses, but you cannot have holes in either nutritional attraction or cover. If you want the deer to move from "Point A" to "Point B," it's critical that you not only give them a reason to do so, but that you establish that reason early enough in the season to make sure that they follow the script at a time when the hunting season is in full swing.

Chapter 19
PREDATORY ACCESS

Huge rubs, large scrapes, and Giant deer tracks filled the 5-acre woodlot...along with zero deer. Night after night, hunts that should have "been," simply weren't. The sign was incredible, chewed-up deer trails littered the forest floor, and the anticipation of youth was always high!

I hunted within a section of land where that 5-acre parcel was located during the late 80's. As a young hunter it was difficult to withstand the temptation to hunt near the explosion of sign. I would often walk ½ mile across the farm fields to get to that small woodlot, wondering where those deer would actually come from to potentially travel by my stand. I remember sitting in my treestand wondering the same thing. Occasionally, a fawn buck would come wandering aimlessly through the woods, but most often my hunts ended without seeing a deer.

I quickly learned the value of not spooking deer on the way to a stand site. "Access", "overall deer/human encounters", and "overuse" was so critical that I began to avoid some of my best stand sites, preferring to give them longer to improve by not using them. Eventually, I would use a stand when the timing was "perfect," meaning that all the considerations of time of year, wind direction, and time of day were optimum. 20 years ago I remember a past hunting partner using a preferred stand of mine on land he trespassed on, stating, "That is too good of a stand not to be used." Did I mention "past" hunting partner?

I have a concept I like to employ on every parcel of land I visit for a client, every portion of public land I hunt, and of course on my own private land hunts that I develop for myself. No matter how many stands you have scattered throughout the landscape, it is often highly advantageous to use what I call, "Perpendicular Access" to not only improve your access through "degrees of movement potential,' but to help you avoid stand overuse, as well as to lower your overall number of deer/human encounters.

Degree Potential of Unspoiled Deer Movements

A rock outcropping juts out high above and in front of the stand, a large and open horse pasture lies out behind the stand, and when you combine those great "pinch point" features with a hidden bedding area around the point to the right, and several hundred yards of cover extending up and to the left towards the food sources...the stage is set for a great hunt! The only thing left to do is to access the "Horse Pasture" stand appropriately, and that can easily be done with "Perpendicular Access." Of course, time of year, time of day, and the type of weather all plays a roll, but by paying attention to perpendicular access my SW WI lease partners and I have used that stand site to kill 6 mature bucks averaging 4 years of age and over 150" of antler growth.

As in most good stand locations, the deer movements typically travel back and forth in front of the stand, as deer move within or between the components of bedding and feeding. In thinking about my personal stand locations on public land in both MI and PA, or on my private land hunting sites in MI or WI, I can't think of a stand site I access that potentially spoils the back and forth movement of the site. In fact, I expect a minimum of a 180-degree window of unspoiled deer hunting potential movements at any stand site or I most likely will not hunt there; and that includes dozens of potential stand sites in the 3 states I currently hunt in. In the Horse Pasture stand that I previously described, my lease partners and I enjoy roughly a 270-degree window of unspoiled deer movements. Topography and perpendicular access combine at the Horse Pasture stand to give us a huge area of deer movement that we can observe as the deer are funneled to within bow range on the upwind side of the stand location. I don't think it's any surprise that our best stand site on our WI lease is also one of the stand sites that features the highest degree of potential, unspoiled deer movements. As the degree potential increases due to perpendicular access...so do your odds for success.

Premature Stand Burn-out

It has long been written that your potential for success decreases each time you access a stand. I have experienced this every year and have planned accordingly - to the extent that over 85% of my mature buck harvests have been killed while using the stand for the first time for the season. Although your odds for success decrease each time you access a stand, that doesn't mean you can't greatly diminish the phenomenon.

When you access a stand site that is perpendicular to deer movements, you rarely place yourself in a position to spook game, especially if care is taken to minimize your "Scent, Site and Sound" while entering and departing your stand. I strongly advocate hunting thin lines of movement whether they be travel corridors, food sources, downwind brush funnels adjacent to heavy bedding cover, etc. When you combine the concept of thin lines of movement with a perpendicular access in which your human presence has been greatly reduced, your negative effect on the stand location overall is kept to a bare minimum.

In my experience there is always a diminishing return on stand usage, meaning, your first sit is at 100% potential, the 2nd less than the first, 3rd less than the 2nd, etc. For the sake of discussion, let's say that poor access might reduce your 2nd sit to a 60% potential, the 3rd sit to a 40% potential, and so on. Now, consider that you take every measure of removing your trace of "Scent, Site, and Sound" from your human intrusion into the woods. Secondly, consider that you have taken every effort to approach with a perpendicular, non-invasive access where you are not exposing yourself to the expected deer movements surrounding the stand site. Sometimes, "not exposing" yourself to the deer movements, may mean the easiest way to access a stand is not the best way. I can honestly say that my typical access to an average stand location in PA, OH, MI and WI, on both public and private lands, takes over ½ hour, 1-way, to reach. The way I personally like to hunt, as well as to make

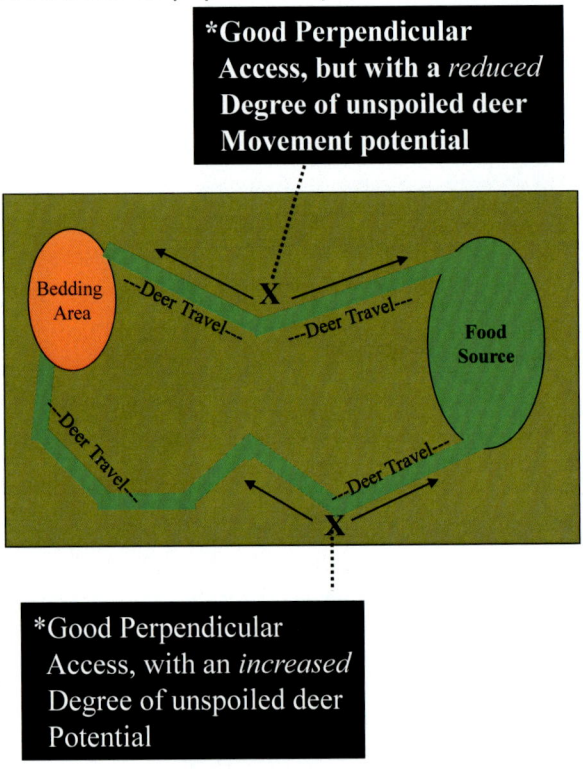

*Good Perpendicular Access, but with a *reduced* Degree of unspoiled deer Movement potential

*Good Perpendicular Access, with an *increased* Degree of unspoiled deer Potential

recommendations for clients to hunt, is that the potential of success for multiple sits in the same stand is much greater if measures are taken to reduce the site, sound and scent of the hunter's approach, a perpendicular access is taken, and the best route to the stand location (not necessarily the easiest route) is taken.

On small private parcels or public land sites where stand locations are potentially fewer, a perpendicular access will help you get the most out of your stand locations by avoiding pre-mature stand burn-out. Can you afford not too? It's not uncommon for quality sits to extend into the 4th or 5th sit if you are doing your best to access the property without the deer even being aware it's hunting season.

Avoiding Deer

Deer are amazing creatures! To me, watching a deer in its natural setting is incredibly relaxing. When a deer feeds, sleeps, travels, and communicates with other deer, I often view it like it's some type of living "puzzle." However, even with my personal obsession for most things "deer," the one thing I avoid at all costs is to actually SEE or SPOOK a deer on the way into my stand sites. I call these "deer/human" encounters, and without getting into too much description, the more encounters you have, the less effective your hunting efforts will ever be. In fact, it's a downward spiral of frequently walking into the woods and telling the deer, "This is when I'm coming, this is where I'm going, this is when I'm leaving, and this is when it's safe for you to come out of hiding." Personally, I want to observe deer where I expect them to be, leave them alone, and make them feel safe until it's the right time, with the right deer, to kill them.

Think of moving about your property like a cougar. For many parcels a cougar could easily drift through a parcel without the deer knowing a predator is nearby. We need to do the same, and although we can't walk as silently as a whisper across dried leaves like a giant cat, we CAN limit how often we potentially expose ourselves to the local deer herd. The way we limit these encounters is by avoiding bedding areas, food sources, and frequent deer hang-outs as we travel about our parcel. But during the months of hunting season, you can take it one step further and attempt to substantially decrease the chances of an encounter at one of the most vulnerable points, your stand location. This is really not that difficult, because all that you have to do is to make sure you are accessing your stand perpendicularly to the travel patterns of the deer that use your parcel, and that you are keeping the deer patterns on the opposite side of the stand from which you enter and exit.

Think of spooking a deer where you hunt as the "tip of the iceberg," meaning the one deer you spooked is a problem that is often reflective of an even bigger problem...the several deer that you didn't even know you spooked because they were a few hundred yards away by the time you arrived at your stand.

Conclusion

Looking back to those learning experiences of the late 80's, I could have often used a perpendicular approach to set up on the downwind side of deer movements and go in for the kill. The problem was that my random movements spooked deer sometimes ¼ mile away before I even reached the woodlot, because I often had to walk right alongside a bedding or feeding area before reaching my stand. Seeing a few deer the first sit turned into zero deer pretty quickly, and I was forced to find other stand locations to try and shoot a deer from. I would venture a guess that my window of degree potential of unspoiled deer movement from that stand location was zero, compared to my SW WI "Horse Pasture" stand of roughly 270 degrees, and the results speak for themselves. Although you will never have the senses and dead-silent movements of a big cat, a perpendicular access is just one more way that you as a hunter can move about your parcel as a more efficient predator.

Chapter 20
STAND STORIES

"Get a soil map, find your best soils on your property, and install your food plots." What do you think of that advice? For tracts of land that include 1000s of acres in TX, or possibly in some of the SE lease country areas, that advice is critical because both efficiency and cost are huge concerns. Even then, the best locations within those "perfect" soil types have to be appropriate, even on very large parcels. However, when we are talking about parcel sizes below 1000 acres, especially smaller than 500, that advice is no different than saying, "Find the coolest looking tree to hang a stand in on your parcel, and go hang a stand in it" with no consideration of deer movements, change in habitat, or access.

I'd like you to take some time to consider all of your stand locations. What kind of story do they have to tell? If it's a short story, you may want to change the location. Every one of your stand locations should tell a story. And before you think I'm totally nuts, "No," I don't typically hear voices from my stand locations - except the variety that came from the nice young couple trespassing through my WI lease in 2010. And wow, I certainly reciprocated a short story of my own prior to their immediate departure. However, if a stand location of yours could talk, could it tell you why it was there in the first place? And how long would the story be? Something to think about is, the longer the story, the better.

Exciting tales of deer movements...the why, when, and where, the spectacular backdrop of a diverse habitat setting, and the predatory approach of camouflaged hunters; what story would your stand site deliver? The longer the story the better, because good things happen in stand locations that have multiple reasons for a deer to walk by!

Deer Trails

Feeding, bedding, and rutting travel patterns can lead to many confusing deer trails that wander throughout the woods. It is critical to understand the purpose of deer travel around your parcel so that you can more closely define your stand locations. What are some of the examples out there for the type of potential stories to be told when it comes to stand placement?

*Feeding trails can be extremely heavy and are a great choice for the early season while deer are still in their summer patterns and haven't fully accepted the fact that it is indeed hunting season! Just keep in mind that as the season progresses, those high deer sightings don't necessarily turn into high buck sightings in the same location. I've witnessed, on several occasions, "pre-rut" mature bucks staying reasonably hidden within fairly decent cover, and traveling several hundred yards on the downwind side of a food source.

*On a paralleling food source trail just inside the woods, the action can be very hot during the pre-rut and rut as bucks are scent-checking the downwind edges for doe activity, as in the example above. However, that same trail can be a pretty poor choice during the early and late season, as the bulk of the herd, even mature bucks, are traveling directly into or out of the food source.

*A trail on the downwind side of a prime bedding area can be an outstanding spot for a morning sneak during the pre-rut, but why stop there? Typically, deer, especially an unpredictable mature buck, have several trails coming in and out of a bedding area which, eventually, all converge to one as the deer take a direct route to or from food sources. The incredible amount of signs on the downwind side of the thicket can be very tempting to sit in; however, pull back and look for where multiple trails converge within close proximity to the bedding area. You can stay away from spooking deer within the bedding area, while at the same time taking advantage of the majority of movements within the area. Keep in mind that, although a pre-rut mature buck might often hang out in his preferred bedding area all day, he will often be extremely active within his core area of safety, making him extremely vulnerable even towards the exterior of his daytime home.

One of my favorite sites involves two converging bedding trails. One hidden bedding bench is high and one is low. Both are roughly 30' in elevation apart and are separated by briars, a very steep drop-off, and rock outcroppings. The two trails converge on the west side, in the "middle", in respect to the elevation of the two bedding areas. By entering from the East, and then south, down a steep face, I can slip into the stand without disturbing deer within their beds to the west in the mid-morning hours after the deer have cleared the fields, and by accessing from downhill in the pre-morning darkness, and then north and up into the stand, the deer don't have to be disturbed while they are feeding out in the open CRP land above. Either way, the stand has been sat in 6 times in 3 years, and only 1 time has there not been a mature buck sighted, with shot opportunities taking place on both 4 and 5 year olds. What also makes the stand work is that the bedding trails run parallel to the upper ag fields, and not to the ag fields. When you have trails leaving bedding areas parallel to the ag fields, that often tells 1 very clear story…a mature buck hot spot! Because of the story these two bedding trails tell at this stand site, it's no wonder why I consider locations like this to provide at least a 33% chance of harvesting a mature buck the first time they are used for the year, after waiting until the appropriate conditions.

Habitat's Splendor

Field edges, various timber transitions, fields, briars, bushes, native grasses, elevation changes, water, and an occasional rock outcropping...how many changes in habitat can you see from your favorite "sit"? "The more, the merrier!" My personal favorites involve traveling benches, distant field edges, timber changes in age or type, and an adjacent bedding area. I think I'd go nuts having to sit in the open hardwoods with no distinct change in habitat. I really get fired up about changes in habitat, and if you don't have habitat changes...make them!

Clear-cut travel corridors, pocket cuttings, and food source edges are all potential "hot-spots;" but why stop there? Blend all 3 together for a can't-miss set up of habitat attraction. Do you need a water source in your area? Add a 55-gallon drum in ½ lengthwise, bury it in the ground a foot below ground level, taper the surrounding soil into a giant funnel above and away from the edges, and you are left with a pretty natural looking water source. What about elevation change? I've actually had a client scoop away dozens of small pockets in ridges the size of a small car throughout an otherwise dead-flat bedding area. By adding shrubs, conifers, and other plantings along the tops of each ridge area, there is now an explosion of habitat change packed into a tiny location.

By providing habitat change to existing habitat diversity, coupled with natural or man-made deer trails, the stage is set for a very long story of deer activity. The only thing left to do is get into a stand site and enjoy!

Camouflaged Access

Wow! I bet as hunters we look kind of funny "sneaking" through the woods pretending to be stealthy. After all, are we really that stealthy even in our best of efforts? And speaking of comical... that reminds me of my latest blunder of washing all of my hunting clothes for an early season hunt, packing all my gear, arriving at my parking spot, and realizing I forgot my hunting pants! Thankfully, a base layer of camo long johns did the trick…and it's truly a shame my tree stand couldn't actually tell the story of some nimrod walking through the fields with green rubber knee boots, tight camo long johns, bow, and the rest of my typical clothing. If only the trees could talk…

We are certainly not a cat, a bear, or even a coyote; however, as humans we can be pretty smart sometimes! So, that means we can see the lay of the land, see how we expose ourselves on a ridgeline or not (hopefully without wearing your long-johns!), and we can bury our site and sounds behind obstructions if planned appropriately. And, of course, our scent…we have the ability to recognize and sometimes even dictate exactly where a deer is bedding and feeding during the daylight in the areas we hunt, so we should be able to effectively navigate around their nose!

Conclusion

How big of a story would your stand location tell you if it could speak? Would it be as dull as a food plot location that was simply installed due to a soil map? How about as ineffective as using all the "really good" trees on the property to hang a stand in? Or, would your stand location spin a lengthy tale of exciting deer movements, the beauty of habitat diversity, and of well-designed predatory sneaks? If you own your own land, create as many stories as possible, and if you don't own your own land, learn to recognize a good read when you see it! The quality of the stories you create prior to the season, most often will determine the level of enjoyment you convey when writing your stories at the end of your season. I like the saying above the door at my old PA deer camp that many of you may recognize, "Hunters, Fisherman and other Liars gather here." Well, the harder you work on your hunting stand story, the more those "lies" will become reality.

23°F ◐ 02/14/12

Chapter 21

THE MORNING SNEAK

The summer of 2005

"Any one hunter who shoots a mature buck in the morning is lucky," the seasoned southern deer manager explained. Well, I was fortunate enough to be sitting in the audience to hear one of my "idols," and I was actually shocked. I remember turning to a friend who had traveled with me hundreds of miles to hear the lineup of distinguished speakers, and his face was displaying the same level of surprise. You see, as a Midwest mature buck hunter I've learned to place a high priority on my pre-rut, late October and early November bow hunts. Although I typically hunt from Mid-September to early January in several states, if priorities dictated, I'd trade the entire season for five morning sits in early November and would still expect success.

A Time of Reflection

Part of my astonishment may have been due to the fact that in the previous season of 2005, I had just arrowed a beautiful five-year-old buck that grossed over 170 inches on an early morning sneak. However, much of my astonishment came from a lifelong of hunting pursuits dating back to 1987 when I missed my first opportunity at a mature buck in the early hours of a misty November morning. Also, that 1987 opportunity was probably reflective of the differences in my hunting experience from that of the famed southern deer manager's. At the time my main hunting grounds were the open agricultural lands of MI's "thumb" area, a region where five and ten acre woodlots were the norm and a ½ mile walk backwards to the woods to shield yourself from the icy December winds, was unfortunately not out of the question. In this typical

Midwest agricultural setting you either got into your stand position with a favorable downwind after a "deer-less" approach before the deer did, or you had an almost impossible task of getting to within bow range later in the day. It was during these seasons of my young hunting career that I experienced the value of morning hunts during the pre-rut of late October and early November, and it was there that I was taught, "The early hunter gets his buck."

The Pattern

That 1987 hunt seems so long ago, but it was the beginning of such a familiar pattern. During the last 20 years the majority of my oldest bucks have had 3 things in common, including: A cool early morning sit with a bow, using the stand for the first time for the year, and hunting during the magical period

The 4th morning of rifle season was a charm for Max in 2006

of pre-rut. In fact, that pattern has been drilled into my hunting experiences for such a long time and so consistently reinforced, that it has become almost an all-consuming year round focus of planning for the next year's morning big buck harvest. The pattern has also turned into such a high percentage of harvest opportunity that I hope you can begin to understand the shock that hit me on that summer day back in 2006 while sitting in an uncomfortable metal chair and listening to some of the experts. Throughout the rest of this article I will convey to you how you too, can experience the success of the morning sneak, and if that famed southern deer manager is reading, I'd like you to know that there just may be a little less luck in hunting mature bucks in the morning than you realize!

Fast Forward

My 2007 scouting season on my SW-WI lease began not much differently than any other year. I left the truck with a partial coating of snow on the ground, a partial roll of orange flagging ribbon in my pocket, and a partial idea of where I wanted my next great morning stand to be. It was a late January afternoon and the snow was at least a week old, which was perfect for eyeballing a collection of established travel patterns, bedding areas, as well as the previous season's rutting activity. I had a bedding area in mind to locate and wanted to find a tree in a downwind funnel to mark for a future stand location. The "set-up" was perfect! The bedding area had much more sign than I thought and was built into a small bench on the SW side of a point that jutted straight south around 300' above the north side of the valley below. A small growth of red cedar filled the SE side of the point, which would make for a good use of screening cover on a future morning sneak. Because of the point and steep face, complete with several rock outcroppings, another bench formed just below and acted as a "double-funnel" for deer to travel along the top of the point, or below on the bench. Where the two travel routes pinched together on the east side of the point, I found the best available tree and flagged it. All that was left was to flag the end of each potential shooting lane where they met a deer trail at the edge of my effective shooting range, and I was out of the area with dreams of a monster whitetail in the early morning hours of the pre-rut.

The stand and shooting lanes were cleared in late spring and by mid-October I was having a very hard time staying away from the stand. My rut hunt during the first full week of November was coming fast, but something happened to change my plans a bit! A cold front was blowing through on October 27th, and I was hopeful that the 20-degree drop in temperature, would reward me with a hastily planned weekend hunt.

The morning sneak was a long one! Over ½ mile of walking across a neighbor's cow pasture, then straight down 200' in elevation, west a ¼ mile, back up to the NW 100', down another 100' to the SW, over 200 yards to the west, and then back up 50' to the NW, followed by a short climb into the best available tree for a stand, an old crooked oak that only allowed me to get 15' in the air. The "best location and best available tree" was going through my mind while I climbed, and to point out that I was a "sweaty mess" would have been an understatement. But, the "ideal" wind direction was stiff out of the NW above, while blowing straight over me and above the hollow below. My downwind was "blocked" by the steep drop and thermals, and I was set for an all-day hunt. Little did I know that the very buck I was hoping for, was getting his picture taken by one of my game cameras above me, roughly 150 yards away!

7:00 rolled around and there was no sign of any deer. 8:00 came and went, 9:00, and by 10:00 I was feeling those lingering doubts we all have experienced. But, the sun was shining brightly, the wind was almost calm at my elevation, and my sweaty undergarments had shed their moisture to the outer layers, to leave me snug and warm. I was also relaxed by the thoughts of all the years of successful morning sneaks, including the majority of my best four and five year old buck encounters. I can even remember a short conversation I shared with a close hunting friend that very morning; "Enjoy the morning! By mid-morning you may be wondering why you didn't choose a different stand, questioning whether you should have gotten out of bed, and sometimes daring to utter the thoughts of 'what a terrible morning'. Then, 20 minutes later you are standing over an expired monster and frankly should have been enjoying the morning all along. You just never know!"

It's taken many years of "slowing down" to be able to enjoy a slow morning, but I was thoroughly enjoying the morning of the 27th and I hadn't even seen a deer yet. Then, as often happens, my wandering thoughts turned into instant anticipation as a flood of excitement sent waves through my entire body. Yep, that was a grunt, deer, and antlers-lots of antlers! They were coming from below and to my east about 50 yards away. The doe and fawn were leading the show and made a sharp turn to come directly at me. It was at this time I felt very fortunate to have taken the time to pile ½ of the debris from clearing my shooting lanes on the "deer-side" base of my tree to keep the deer away from a steep-angled shot, and away from any lingering scent left over from climbing into the tree. Of course, the other ½ of the brush, I took great care in placing at my furthest shooting points and beyond, to effectively "pinch" the deer travel into the sweet spot of 10-25 yards, and those does were following the script.

The does continued towards my tree, angled up and to the NW around the brush and past the tree, and then stopped somewhere behind my left shoulder. With a quick grunt the buck began to follow, and to my relief, I heard the doe and fawn move "un-spooked" away. Now, I'm not one of those guys who come back to camp to tell you about the 15 pointer they couldn't get a shot at. Instead, I'm one of those guys that make a split-second decision of "shooter or not," and gets ready for the shot. I thought maybe the buck was a nice 3-year-old 12-point that we had numerous pictures of, but I was worried more about the shot on an obvious shooter then mentally measuring his G2s! The buck came closer and closer, and finally paused long enough at 15' to get a shot. Little did I know he was indeed the 5-year-old buck I was dreaming about, and he actually did have 15 scorable points!

Conclusion

Was this just another buck story? I guess in some respects it was, but I ask you to consider the carefully constructed plan that was both predictable and realistic. The stand was located downwind of a great bedding area with deer-less approach and a potential downwind blocker due to topography. The access to the stand was screened from the bedding area and covered two funnels that converged into one. The agricultural field and plantings were 150 yards away, and the photo of the buck at the edge of that field while I was entering the stand, was proof that my very difficult approach that was well below the large feeding area, was worth the effort. The stand location was also saved for the perfect time of the year and hadn't been accessed since installation. The perfect wind, the perfect morning, and the perfect Midwest agricultural hunting pattern that fits like an old familiar glove, had been repeated yet again, and I can't tell you how much passion I have for planning my annual morning sneaks!

Over the seasons I've learned to save the best of my morning stands adjacent to bedding areas for the pre-rut when bucks seem to get back to their favorite daylight hang-outs just a little bit later. Some of these stands I sit in once a year, some twice, and some of my favorites go un-touched, as the conditions never become favorable for the perfect morning sneak. However, when the conditions are right and the stand has been preserved, you haven't only planned for success, you expect success and get excited about it, because in my experience there is not a more predictable outcome when hunting the mature monarchs of the Midwest. And, if you happen to lack the experience of shooting big bucks in the morning with a bow, spend a little more seat time in a Midwest morning treestand, where careful planning will lead to a pattern of predictable success.

Chapter 22
CONCLUSION

The crosshairs settled on his front left shoulder as the buck stopped, stared, and stood motionless as my panicked inner emotions turned into a slow-motioned pace of subtle physical movements. The gun was already pointed out the window with my left elbow resting on my thigh, and my "auto-pilot" kicked in for the final 3 steps of "Safety Off," "Aim Small" and "Squeeze Slowly." The "BOOM" of the .270 WSM that broke the morning chill was extremely loud and full of excitement. Through a haze of slight smoke, a whirl of white and brown disappeared within an instant, and except for a breaking branch to my left and away, the woods turned back into its peaceful morning silence.

Zero blood and zero hair turned into a ½ hour ever-increasing pattern of ½ circle searches to the southeast, combined with an ever-increasing sense of hopelessness. ½ circle patterns turned into walking out the 3 main runs through the thick northern lowland, and the spot of blood 100 yards into the swamp made my heart pound full of hope. Only 20' away the 4-year old 148" northern monarch had expired in his brushed choked escape route, and I could quickly see he was the biggest buck I had harvested on any of the MI lands that I had ever hunted, let alone on public land!

And **where** that buck was shot is the surprise! My 2011 Public Land buck was a great buck that offered a great hunting adventure, and he was a product of an overall design of hunting concepts that I use anywhere I hunt; even on public land. During this hunt I used a "Predatory Access" to approach perpendicular to the "Line of Movement" that was between bedding and feeding, and into a line of "Screening Cover" that hid my movements to the outside. The "Depth of Cover" was approximately 1 ½ miles long as the buck no doubt targeted the numerous October and November bait piles that anchored one end of his line of movement, while the remote, and hunter-less "High Stem Count per Acre" bedding cover anchored the other end. My blind location told multiple "Stand Stories" of various habitat changes in the form of open marsh, dark swamp, and water, while at the same time being adjacent to a northern conifer mix of "High Powered Cool Season Bedding Cover." Unlike the nighttime hunting season food sources over a mile away that included deer blinds, trucks, talking, human scent and bait piles, the daytime area he chose to call home was within the most "Stress Free" habitat he could find. After hunting this area for well over a decade, I learned quite a few things; one of those being, to rarely expect to see a doe in these locations. This was a true "mature buck area," well behind and away from the human and doe family group stressors, that on November 17, 2011, this buck obviously chose to stay away from.

Public land or private, I have enjoyed experiencing the concepts of Whitetail Success that I have shared with you in this book. The concepts and ideas in this book are based on my own personal experiences. 27 years ago my brother and I started hunting whitetails under the tutelage of any hunting magazine we could get our hands on. We were so "green" that when I shot my first deer with an arrow at the age of 16, I had to rely on the folded "10 easy steps to field dressing a deer" from my pocket, while my brother "dry-heaved" off to the side. I didn't know a heart from a liver, and just like in deer hunting, I had to figure it out through experience as I scouted the public and private lands of my early whitetail pursuits.

Reflecting on the past 27 years, it has been an incredible experience to be able to piece together the various concepts that have been a consistent theme throughout my hunting opportunities. To be able to take those consistencies, and to then be able to apply them to not only my own whitetail pursuits in numerous states, but to those of my clients, my beliefs and ideas have been able to be continually experienced and reinforced. These are the concepts that have worked for me anywhere I have hunted or managed whitetail deer. I have found my experiences to be applicable to any piece of whitetail habitat I have had the privilege of scouting, hunting, and working on. What I want you to take from this book is the excitement that I have enjoyed while employing these ideas during the lifelong pursuit of designing my own personal level of Whitetail Success. There is often more than 1 way to accomplish a task and that is no different in the pursuit of whitetail deer, but these concepts have defined how I have experienced Whitetail Success for decades in the past, and hope to in the decades yet to come. I personally rely on these concepts of Whitetail Design, and I am excited for you as a brother in hunting, to do the same! Whether you hunt private land and use these concepts to build your success, or you hunt public land and use these concepts to find your success, I believe that these concepts can help you design your next whitetail hunt of a lifetime.

176

ORDER MORE BOOKS OR SERVICES HERE!

*Whitetail Success by Design makes a great gift for someone else, or for yourself. Simply include the quantity of books needed and any special shipping instructions.

☐ Qty.

*If you would like Jeff to contact you to discuss the opportunities for any of the services he offers listed below he would be happy to do so:

☐ 1. Site visit to your land to create a plan for your hunting and habitat design.

☐ 2. Site visit to your land to complete habitat improvement projects, including building bedding areas, creating travel corridors, container waterhole installations and more!

☐ 3. Site visit to public land with you to design a hunting strategy.

☐ 4. To facilitate your next Whitetail Event, including Habitat Days, Hunter Banquets, Workshops or Educational Events.

-Request a book(s) to be sent to the following address(es):

_____
Name

_____
Street Address

_____
City, State, Zip

_____
Email

Additional shipping addresses:

_____
Name

_____
Street Address

_____
City, State, Zip

_____
Email

_____
Name

_____
Street Address

_____
City, State, Zip

_____
Email

_____
Name

_____
Street Address

_____
City, State, Zip

_____
Email

_____
Name

_____
Street Address

_____
City, State, Zip

_____
Email

ORDER MORE BOOKS OR SERVICES HERE!

*Whitetail Success by Design makes a great gift for someone else, or for yourself. Simply include the quantity of books needed and any special shipping instructions.

☐ Qty.

*If you would like Jeff to contact you to discuss the opportunities for any of the services he offers listed below he would be happy to do so:

☐ 1. Site visit to your land to create a plan for your hunting and habitat design.

☐ 2. Site visit to your land to complete habitat improvement projects, including building bedding areas, creating travel corridors, container waterhole installations and more!

☐ 3. Site visit to public land with you to design a hunting strategy.

☐ 4. To facilitate your next Whitetail Event, including Habitat Days, Hunter Banquets, Workshops or Educational Events.

-Request a book(s) to be sent to the following address(s):

_____
Name

_____
Street Address

_____
City, State, Zip

_____
Email

Additional shipping addresses:

_____
Name

_____
Street Address

_____
City, State, Zip

_____
Email

_____
Name

_____
Street Address

_____
City, State, Zip

_____
Email

_____
Name

_____
Street Address

_____
City, State, Zip

_____
Email

_____
Name

_____
Street Address

_____
City, State, Zip

_____
Email

ORDER MORE BOOKS OR SERVICES HERE!

*Whitetail Success by Design makes a great gift for someone else, or for yourself. Simply include the quantity of books needed and any special shipping instructions.

☐ Qty.

*If you would like Jeff to contact you to discuss the opportunities for any of the services he offers listed below he would be happy to do so:

☐ 1. Site visit to your land to create a plan for your hunting and habitat design.

☐ 2. Site visit to your land to complete habitat improvement projects, including building bedding areas, creating travel corridors, container waterhole installations and more!

☐ 3. Site visit to public land with you to design a hunting strategy.

☐ 4. To facilitate your next Whitetail Event, including Habitat Days, Hunter Banquets, Workshops or Educational Events.

-Request a book(s) to be sent to the following address(s):

_____
Name
_____
Street Address
_____
City, State, Zip
_____
Email

Additional shipping addresses:

Name

Street Address

City, State, Zip

Email

Name

Street Address

City, State, Zip

Email

Name

Street Address

City, State, Zip

Email

Name

Street Address

City, State, Zip

Email

ORDER MORE BOOKS OR SERVICES HERE!

*Whitetail Success by Design makes a great gift for someone else, or for yourself. Simply include the quantity of books needed and any special shipping instructions.

☐ Qty.

*If you would like Jeff to contact you to discuss the opportunities for any of the services he offers listed below he would be happy to do so:

☐ 1. Site visit to your land to create a plan for your hunting and habitat design.

☐ 2. Site visit to your land to complete habitat improvement projects, including building bedding areas, creating travel corridors, container waterhole installations and more!

☐ 3. Site visit to public land with you to design a hunting strategy.

☐ 4. To facilitate your next Whitetail Event, including Habitat Days, Hunter Banquets, Workshops or Educational Events.

-Request a book(s) to be sent to the following address(es):

_____
Name
_____
Street Address
_____
City, State, Zip
_____
Email

Additional shipping addresses:

_____
Name

_____
Street Address

_____
City, State, Zip

_____
Email

_____
Name

_____
Street Address

_____
City, State, Zip

_____
Email

_____
Name

_____
Street Address

_____
City, State, Zip

_____
Email

_____
Name

_____
Street Address

_____
City, State, Zip

_____
Email